BOBBE
BAGGIO,
PH.D.

#WFH
WORK FROM HOME

EVERYDAY REFLECTIONS ON COVID-19 AND THE
REMOTE WORKPLACE

First Edition: 2021

ISBN: 978-0-9914051-6-9

Ebook and Print Interior Design by Steven W. Booth,
    www.GeniusBookServices.com

Cover Design by Senhor Tocas, www.SenhorTocasIllustrator.tumblr.com

Table of Contents

#WFH Work From Home

Fast Foreword

This book explores the impact of #WFH (work from home) on regular people, everyday lives and the way we work and feel. A pandemic started in China in early February 2020 when cities like Huanggang and Wuhan sent workers home and the province of Hubei went on lockdown. China is where COVID-19 originated and in China working from home was almost unheard of prior to the pandemic. But once the government shut everything down and encouraged workers to stay at home, millions of Chinese started to experience the pros and cons of working from home for the first time. Much like the scenes in New York that were to follow, early on the streets in Beijing, Shanghai and Guangzhou were spooky and quiet. Videoconference platforms took the place of conference tables and WeChat, DingTalk and Zoom were being used everywhere. Workers around the globe have had to adjust to a new way of working. Bosses have had to adjust to a new way of trusting. Individuals have had to reconsider what and how they focus: are they distracted by family members and finding it difficult to concentrate or are they enjoying the experience and improving their productivity? Everyone has been forced to adapt.

We are slowly starting to see work as something other than clocking in and out. There has been a resurgence in monitoring applications even though all research shows that watching remote employees doesn't make them more productive; if anything, just the opposite occurs. Bosses are beginning to admit that working from home makes workers more efficient. Internal ways of working are being adjusted to accommodate a remote work force. Families are spending more time together, less time commuting and even earth's atmosphere is benefitting. But it is not all easy. Prior to COVID-19 about 43% of the U.S. workforce worked remotely, at least some of the time, according to Gallop. Workplace cultures, whether in the U.S. or China or most other countries, change slowly. Standard administration policies and procedures just don't translate well to the remote workplace, and with the exception of technology and creative agencies, employers have a long way to go to feel really comfortable.

It always comes back to trust and control. When employees respond to emails or texts late, or take time for personal things, or miss a meeting, it can make administration feel uneasy. Weekly meetings, daily meeting and impromptu meetings can make them feel like they are more connected, and everyone is on the same page. Daily reporting on what employees have done, what they plan on doing tomorrow, and what they are doing today is also often required. These are evidence of the "trust gap." Often, it might make administration feel better, but it doesn't usually work out well with employees. More time in meaningless meetings cuts into time for real work. Reporting daily achievements and tomorrow's tasks takes time. Workers think it decreases efficiency and increases unnecessary time.

Most companies have the essential technologies for working from home but it's not about that. It's about decreasing the office rent expenditure and long commute time, increasing time with family and quality of life. For working from home to be successful, the remote worker has to learn how to effectively balance work and life. Often people initially feel more stressed both mentally and physically. Once people adjust, they tend to like working from home; balancing work and life can be rewarding and decrease stress. More traditional industries, production floor workers and teams that require a high degree of coordination will still be averse to working from home. The new normal is helping people see that it's time to change and open up to new possibilities. Old habits are difficult to change but the old style of management is becoming less popular. Companies are focusing more on what employees need and how they can contribute. #WFH has forced companies to examine relationships and elevate their culture to include trust and to care more about employees.

It happened overnight. One week in mid-March 2020, Silicon Valley let over 500,000 employees go home to work. That was only the beginning. COVID-19 has had a significant impact on businesses, customers and all aspects of our lives. It took us by surprise. According to research conducted by RavenIntel.com in April 2020, 51% of businesses had been drastically impacted by COVID-19 and only 2% had not been impacted at all. More than half of businesses felt that the impact would be long term, greater than six months or more. Projects had been delayed, purchases had been postponed and workplace changes had accelerated. More than 63% of businesses reported that working from home has made them more productive. Almost everyone is and will be focused on the impact of COVID-19 and working from home for a long time. Many businesses possessed the equipment, software and connections needed for people to work from home prior to the pandemic, but they never did it. Partly because of organizational culture and partly because of the human need for connection and proximity, working from home was not an option for most companies. Now it is the "new normal" and many organizations are moving forward and not looking back. There is a lot to learn and a lot that will make us all stronger and better once we come out of this on the other side. Hopefully, company cultures will change to embrace the positives and allow their employees the flexibility to work remotely on a regular basis.

Going virtual overnight has proven that we can work remotely and do it effectively. COVID-19 has forced a new reality. Connection in the remote workplace requires more effort and everyone working together, not in silos. Remote work requires knowledge sharing, leadership and regular

What the... Happened?

communications. Strategic decisions, plans and projects require engagement, clear expectations and setting individual priorities based on business values. It's a big change for most workers. The systems and structures need to be adapted, and organizational hierarchies adjusted, to a much flatter workplace.

Quick decision making and communications around plans has proven itself to be paramount. Companies obsessed with process and procedure have been flung into a new world. Even if it is not positive or good news, everyone wants to know what is going on. And they want a plan, NOW. Knowing what is happening and when allows people to make decisions that impact their personal situation. This is not to say that the organization's decisions can't change but constant pivoting causes stress, anxiety and tension. Good leadership is paramount in any crisis. This is a crisis like we have never seen. It will have long term impact on all aspects of our lives including legal, academic, healthcare, leisure and commerce.

Many pioneers and evangelists have been singing the praises of remote work for decades. Finally, the rest of the world is starting to catch on. It saves on time, gasoline and pollution. It allows companies to utilize global talent resources, save on rent and utility bills and gives people the opportunity to cut out the commute. Most companies have adapted very quickly and successfully, but for some it has been more difficult. For companies connected by a shared passion and vision, not just by physical presence, it has been easier. Having everyone on the same page and knowing what "true north" looks like helps. #WFH is a dramatic change in organizational design and experience. There is an integral magic that happens when people come together in an office environment to create, design and contribute, or so they imagine. There is also a long history and stereotypes that pigeonhole engineers and programmers as benefiting from remote work but not process and production people. When organizations have been successful doing something one way for a long time, it's hard to change.

Look at education for example. Much of what happens in K-12 and Higher Education is based on precedent not improvement. Prior to 2011 and the advent of 3G, the world really had little other choice. Business, education, and almost everything in the economy was built on person-to-person connections. Once we got the internet and finally got an upgraded broadband connection that allowed us to communicate across boundaries easily, it was a matter of pattern. Human beings like to stick to what they know. We like our comfort zones.

Working in an environment that requires no physical presence requires mental and emotional adjustments. It removes a ton of unconscious bias and puts the focus on results. Most people feel like they are more productive working from home. It is less about the color of your skin, the clothes you wear or the way you sound and show up and more about your work. It requires the individual to be more self-reflective because there is less immediate verification of validity from peers. There are emotional repercussions to doing it all: working, childcare, schooling and your own self-care. Even the CEO of Cisco said in the New York Times on March 29, 2020 that "as much as we sell this to our customers, I'm not sure I want to do it 100 percent of the time."

Everything takes a little more thought, a little more effort and a little more reflection. It also takes confidence and trust by employees and employers. Communications that are meaningful and effective are everything when you work remotely. You need clear expectations, verification and feedback. This requires managers and executives to trust, to clarify and to communicate exactly what is expected of the worker. It requires everyone to be focused, aware and engaged.

Certainly, the pace of change has been impacted almost overnight. How we work, where we work and when we work has changed. Large segments of the economy have gone home to work, while juggling homeschooling and space sharing. COVID-19 has accelerated one of the greatest workplace transformations ever. It has sent unemployment rates soaring and triggered uncertainty. Human Resources (HR) managers and Training and Development (T&D) specialists are scurrying to ramp up training on the effective remote workplace. They are creating coaching courses, guides and worker and management training. Working from home has taken the emphasis off of physical space and centered it on worker well-being. Well-being is no longer a "perk"; it is essential. Some workers feel like they have been hit by a tsunami and others feel relief. Most understand this is a revolution where there is no going back. The new normal will not be "normal."

Many people actually say they can get a lot more work done in the remote workplace. They have less interruptions and more concentration. They can be as efficient or more efficient and work half the time. They are not wasting time talking, socializing and gossiping. So much of the workday was previously filled up with unproductive activities and not focused on results. Many say they feel like they are working more, putting in longer hours at home. They feel like they can't shut it off. Their "on-button" is stuck "on." Probably the biggest impact is how productivity will be measured. It can't be measured by going in early and staying late. If you go in early and stay late, it doesn't matter. What matters is the result. Each individual will have not only a unique workspace, but a unique optimum schedule. The workday will certainly become more flexible. As people create their own workspaces at home, not for temporary work but for the long term, ergonomics and remote labor laws will change. Many compliance laws are written exclusively for the traditional work environment. Who provides what and who pays for it will also change. Very few states have laws specifically governing the remote work environment.

Of all the industries effected, technology was the most comfortable and most ready. They were used to connections, security and computers. But even companies like Microsoft had to adjust. Spotty internet service doesn't care who you are. Sheltering in place and sending everyone home has highlighted these areas also. It is a big adjustment for people who are not used to #WFH. Coping with your inner circle all day can be very trying. Whether it is a partner, spouse or children, or maybe aging parents, they are much closer now for most of the day. The sheer volume of communications via text, apps, phone and email has skyrocketed. More people are meditating because more people need to. Many folks are experiencing mental health challenges.

They are also learning what it means to "Act with Autonomy" and to be able to "Set and Enact Priorities," two of the essential respond-abilities spelled out in The Pajama Effect, a book I wrote about the remote workplace in 2014. People are adapting as best they can. There are tradeoffs. There is a considerable amount of stress. And they are struggling with change and balance: with the new and the old, with personal life and work life, and with the flexibility and freedom of the remote workplace contrasted with new expectations and trust. The new HQ is home.

It is the beginning of March 2020 and the world is starting to wake up to the enormous threat of COVID-19. China is already struggling, and Italy is under siege. Up until now the United States has not really taken this threat seriously and preemptive measures have been ignored. And then it happens. High Tech announces nearly overnight that everyone is going home. The Silicon Valley and the Washington State Technology Sector will close because of the Coronavirus and the world of work as we know it will never be the same again. Microsoft sends 54,000 staff members home, Apple sends 12,000, Facebook sends 17,000, and between the three almost 83,000 workers are told not to come in on Friday, but to work from home. The offices will remain open for now but the workers are to work virtually from their homes. Workers are told to stay away from the office and all business trips are cancelled. Facebook had already closed the Seattle office when a contractor there reportedly was infected with COVID-19. Microsoft tells the San Francisco Bay area and Seattle workers to stay home. The Seattle HQ houses about 54,000 workers and approximately a third of the global staff. They agree to continue to pay hourly workers even if they cannot come to work. California is one of the few states that has remote working compliance laws. Google is asking people who can work from home to do so, and Amazon confirms that an employee at their HQ in Seattle has also tested positive for the coronavirus. The state of California issues a state of emergency. The death toll from COVID-19 in the United States increases to 15 and the number of reported cases rises to 250.

Chapter 2

Virtually Overnight

Apple retail stores remain open for now and the work from home offer is extended to most of the global organization. Facebook confirms that their offices will remain closed until at least March 9, which will eventually turn in to the rest of 2020 and probably well beyond. Microsoft has more than 80,000 workers across the country. Google urges nearly 100,000 across the U.S. and Canada to work remotely. Amazon gives the green light for more than 50,000 to work remotely. High Tech focuses on the health and welfare of their workers with the confidence that remote work is not only possible, but they are well prepared for the proposition.

Public health officials are recommending that large gatherings be minimized, and the phrase "social distancing" enters our vocabulary. The fear of spreading COVID-19 and health concerns for team members and their families causes us to take drastic measures to "flatten the curve." Employees, except those critical to security and safety, are told to work remotely. It will not be long before other sectors will follow suit and entire states and most of the economy will essentially close. Nothing like anything we have seen in our lifetimes, COVID-19 will close everything except essential businesses and create a new way of looking at work that has been possible but resisted for years.

Since the world went 4G in 2011, working from home has been more than possible for much of the economy. Many people work with computers all day, and as the technology has evolved both synchronous and asynchronous platforms made connections to the remote workplace better and more accessible. Video chat platforms are everywhere and the ability to meet and conduct business is convenient and easy. Then, in 2020, the resistance to working from home changed overnight. Issues of trust, control and influence were transformed by the necessity to keep people safe. Those who could work from home did it.

It started with large employers in the sector that was the readiest to go: Large tech companies that had the equipment, the portals, the cloud, and the connectivity led the way to the remote workplace. For many employees, working from home (#WFH) was an alternative to not safe for work (#NSFW). How workers conducted their daily affairs was not all that different. The companies had set up a portal so that once workers signed into their computers, the office looked pretty much the same.

Then the remote work offer got extended. Microsoft decided that anyone worldwide who could work from home really needed to do so. Everyone was to stay home until at least March 25th. To make the workplace safer for everyone, those people who had to go into the office would continue to go to their work locations, but the offices would be sanitized, and government guidelines would be followed.

Next, the terms essential and non-essential workers transformed a thriving economy into a new world. One that was broken, different and headed for economic recession. Those people who could work from home were the lucky ones, they would continue to produce and continue to get paid. Those companies that were ready for this, and understood the remote work environment and supported their employees, were also fortunate. Not everyone was so lucky. Corporate headquarters in the shape of spaceships and billions of dollars' worth of office real estate would remain empty for quite a while.

It took a long time for the United States to react. China initially announced the spread of COVID-19 in early January and President Trump decided to close travel and initiated a coronavirus task force on January 29, 2020. FEMA was put in charge of securing medical supplies until mid-March but the CDC (Center for Disease Control) was essentially ignored and muffled. The White House did not trust the CDC and the CDC did not trust the White House. By mid-May, the White House would try to shut down the CDC. With the economy headed for a severe recession and an election looming on the horizon, political interests were being put in front of the public health and welfare. *The New York Times* analyzed that more than 380,000 people arrived in the U.S. from China in January, including around 4,000 from Wuhan. After the restrictions began, almost 40,000 people arrived in the U.S. from China in February and March.

By the end of March, much of the economy in the United States had ground to a halt because of state restrictions and the continued escalation and spread of the virus. Non-essential workers were restricted from going to the office. Entire sectors of the economy would remain closed for months. New York, California, Pennsylvania, and other large states ordered most businesses to close. Millions of workers were sent home and millions of people were out of work as many states issued orders that people were to stay inside. Some business was exempt, including financial institutions, some retailers, pharmacies, hospitals, manufacturing plants and transportation companies. Non-essential work and meetings of any size and for any reason were restricted. The economy was closed except for those that were deemed essential or could work from home.

Schools and the education system were, for all intents and purposes, shut down as districts scrambled to establish connectivity and equal access for all K-12 students. Then there was the matter of learning. K-12 education was about to find out that remote access and online learning are not the same thing. Higher Education was thrust into a state of emergency remote teaching. A sector that had resisted online learning for decades, regardless of the research, suddenly had no other choice. Students were going home for spring break and not coming back. Faculty threw online schooling together as quickly as possible with little understanding and almost no guidance. Higher Education and K-12 were about to discover that there is a huge difference between emergency remote teaching and online learning. Well-planned and designed online learning experiences are vastly different from courses offered online in response to a crisis or disaster. Colleges and universities were given no other option. K-12 wasn't either. Even those schools known as 1 to 1 schools, where students all had Chromebooks or computers and internet access, were about to learn how really underprepared they were to go online.

Most of the Higher Education sector was not prepared, and implementing online learning, even with support, is not an overnight process. Higher Education was facing unprecedented decisions and scrambling to keep students, faculty, and staff safe during a public health emergency. Many institutions canceled all their face-to-face classes and ordered faculty to put everything online to help stop the spread of the virus. Institutions of all different sizes and statures suddenly had to stop debating the value of remote learning and had to start doing it. Everyone was moving their courses and learning experiences online. Many instructors were stressed and much of what was being created was a quick fix solution. Online learning has been a very political term in Higher Education for decades. This scramble to go remote and the lack of knowledge about what good online experiences are all about certainly created a political climate that offered diverse solutions and mixed teaching practices. This rush to produce remote learning without the planning, knowledge and support needed to do it well was a prescription for problems.

For much of Higher Education, learning stopped in mid-March. Students went home for spring break with the idea they would return and then were told not to come back to campus. The same scenario played out in K-12. Teachers thought they were being sent home for a few weeks and then were told not to return. At first learning was put on hold, with the idea of reviewing what had already been covered. Then it became clear that emergency remote teaching was the mode we would be in for the rest of the school year. The term emergency remote teaching has emerged in education circles to describe what has been advocated for as a solution to the public health crisis of COVID-19 versus the development of quality online learning environments. Not all the options or solutions are equally effective and not all the institutions have been able to implement remote emergency teaching by delivering the same type and quality of learning.

Even with connectivity tools like Zoom, Chromebooks and ClassDojo in place, few teachers were ready to finish out the school year online. School districts scrambled to assure equal access, internet connections, hardware and software, and of course accessibility. Parents were now full-time teachers and remote learning was homeschooling. By April 10, 2020, 124,000 schools had been closed and about 55 million students affected. As schools rushed to shift education online using emergency remote teaching, concerns developed about absenteeism, special needs students, technology, grading, and school meals. For a whole host of reasons, many districts decided to do nothing and put the rest of the term on hold, and then try to pick up again the next school year. That led to debating whether to give the grades students earned by March as the final grade. Even the Ivy League cancelled classes and closed dorms. The U.S. Department of Education put a hold on loan repayment and standardized testing was either eliminated, put online or put on hold.

In February, unemployment hovered around 5.8 million; by April, 23 million Americans were without work. The economy contracted 4.8 percent from January to March 2020 and the unemployment rate increased to 14.7% by April. Economists indicated that most of the economic impact came from mandatory shutdowns. States issued stay at home orders somewhere between March 15 and March 21, starting with California, followed by most of the Northeast and some of the Northwest by March 28, and much of the middle of the country straggled in by early April. Stay at home orders encouraged residents to stay home, unless they were essential workers (such as medical care, drug store and grocery personnel, etc.) The state of New York directed that non-essential employees of any kind must work from home. By April 2, about 90% of the U.S. population was under restraint.

Evangelists for the remote workplace and distance learning are hoping that this emergency will propel those who have been resistant into the 21st century to join the bandwagon and open pathways where there had previously been resistance. Others are genuinely concerned that the thrust into remote workplaces will have a backlash that will make this move even more difficult in the long run. The United States had some previous experience with mass emergency education and displaced workers with Hurricane Katrina in 2005 but that was nothing like the spring of 2020. By the summer of 2020, over a million people had been infected with the virus and where and how people would work or go to school in the future was still unanswered.

By the summer 2020, everyone who could stay home was told to do so. Remote working was here to stay at least for the foreseeable future. People were confused, and felt the information they were receiving was untrustworthy, unreliable, false or misleading. Political jargon on both sides of the aisle ran rampant. Protests made international news. Governors were under pressure to open up state economies and some did. States reopened too soon, and the virus came back with a vengeance. There was no question the economy had taken a hit, a hard hit. People were confused, frightened and unsure. High Tech announced that everyone would work from home for the rest of the year and some companies like Nationwide Insurance decided that working from home was saving the company so much money and was so effective, it is a practice that will permanently continue.

The deaths from the pandemic were higher in early summer of 2020 than all the deaths from the Vietnam and Korean Wars combined. They had even surpassed the deaths from World War I. People were afraid and people were staying at home. Even as small business began to reopen, restrictions limited business activities. Everything had been affected from public transportation to prisons, nursing homes, and hospitals. Event cancellations impacted sports and religious services. Even the opioid crisis had been touched by the virus, and cases have increased. Gun sales increased, and the crime rate across the country increased including murders and suicides. The impact on education caused a crisis that remains unresolved. Some schools were determined to return to campus in the fall; others vowed to stay online and remote.

The virus shut down Broadway and major league baseball. Basketball's March Madness was cancelled and the future of football in the fall remained uncertain. Many large events like the U.S. Open decided to go virtual and broadcast the event without anyone in the stands. The National Hockey League was cancelled, and the National Basketball League was too. They would eventually resume without fans in the stands. College athletics were halted in the spring and the fall had a scattered and mixed approach. The media was broadcasting from people's homes using Zoom and Facetime and playing a lot of repeats. The shutdown impacted streaming services and syndicated programs alike.

By mid-summer, work in the United States and around the globe looked quite different than it had a year before. When people left the traditional workplace and went home varied by industry, but certainly by early spring everyone who could make that decision was on board with it. Some would return to the workplace; others would remain at home.

This book is the study of different individuals from a variety of industries across the United States. It reflects their perspectives on early COVID-19 and then six months after the initial shock of #WFH. These are real people. Some were prepared. Some were not. Some like #WFH, and some don't. Regardless, everyone's life has been changed forever.

Chapter 3

Are You Ready for This?

Neal

When I interviewed Neal in early April 2020, for Neal working from home was nothing new. Neal is a consultant who has been working from home for a long time. "Twenty-five years ago I literally took my hat off and I was done in the corporate world. I find that the independence of working from home and the freedom of doing what I need to do, when I need to do it, fits my personality exactly. It takes a certain discipline in your life to be more productive. What this crazy coronavirus has done is shut down my social life. I enjoy having lunch with colleagues and meeting for business deals. But I don't think I would ever want to go back inside the corporate office permanently, not ever again."

Neal works with clients in many different industries and channels. When asked about his clients, and whether they were ready for this, the first example he gave was a well-established construction firm in Northern California. He said, "I had a genuinely nice conversation with the CEO who put everything on hold. The construction business was hit hard. They were not prepared for this. Everyone, everywhere wants construction back up and running as soon as possible, even the governor."

Neal did come up with a plan and introduced his clients to Microsoft Teams where they could meet, and they began talking daily. To keep the social connections going they developed game nights where they played poker. When Neal asked them, they indicated they planned on keeping those poker nights going even after the pandemic ended because it brought people together. Neal said the construction company did a good job of adapting, working with what they had and keeping up the people-to-people connections that are so critical to business success. They thought talking daily with Microsoft Teams brought a more personalized perspective to their workforce than they had ever had before. This small construction firm seemed to adapt well and quickly.

It was not the same experience he had with larger enterprises. With them, there seemed to be a sense of anxiety, of wanting to go back to "normal" even though normal was not working all that well. It was what they knew, and it was comfortable. Some people are not working, some are working harder than they ever have. It's the familiarity of coming down the hall to talk to the boss or a colleague or HR that they miss. These folks are not happy at all. But when Neal asked the question, "Do you think there will be changes within the organization after this is over?" The response he got was, "No, we want to go right back to where we were before this happened." Neal thinks it will take at least one if not more than one more incident to get older, larger companies to change.

Throwing new technology at companies in an attempt to initiate change has not worked. People say the technology is confusing, "I do not know how to use it, I do not know how to get to it. Zoom is not the answer, nor is any other piece of technology." Some businesses have not adapted well at all. The people Neal talked to indicated the challenge was not organizing themselves, but the mass of confusion they had to deal with inside the organization. It is not so much that these folks do not want to change, it is about the inexperience within the organization of how to make change happen. People are stuck. They ask: "Do I react? Am I proactive? And if I volunteer is it going to fall right back on me?" This is a classic reaction from an organization that is large, structured and governed by process and procedure when asked to make a big change in how they do things. They just can't make it happen.

Neal finds that when he works from home having a consistent schedule helps. Neal started categorizing his time on a calendar so he could see where he is spending his time. He keeps a regular schedule where he gets up at 4:30 AM and is in the "office" by 7 AM. He tries to keep up the discipline of setting himself up like he was "going to the office" every day.

In Neal's opinion, most companies are not ready for the remote workplace. "You have to understand what your business is and that not everything can be done remotely. But the big stumbling block is defining your tasks and knowing what can be done remotely. The workplace mentality says if any of it must be done in the office, it all has to be done there." Human Resources is often distanced from the workforce. HR is usually centralized and detached. In the few cases that HR is positioned in the regional organization, it would be possible for them to act as a change agent and support the remote workplace. Usually though, it is centralized and removed.

Then there is the issue of trust. HR needs to rewrite and redo evaluations, compliance, performance reviews, etc. so that they reflect not just your performance goal but also your impact on the rest of the organization. We are going to reward you, pay you and promote you based on deliverables and it really does not matter where you are. HR could and should make a huge difference in the adoption of trust, supporting people being remote and changing the old thought process that if I am not in the office, "I am being overlooked."

According to Neal, organizations should lose the annual performance review and make it more frequent: quarterly, monthly, or even weekly. This is especially important for remote workers. The frequency is not as important as the parameters. Lose the cascading goals and write it in clear terms. It is difficult to get rid of the old performance management mindset because it is how senior managers check on productivity, even though there is truly little relationship. We need clearer expectations and quality control measures instead of performance management. Organizations use the term "optics," which means watching over the workforce, which is ridiculous. It signifies old-fashioned, low level, outdated worker and management relationships that no longer serve anyone. It is a 150-year-old tradition that organizations need to lose now. Give people the tools they need and let them do the work. The ones that are motivated will, and those are the folks you want working for you.

Neal thinks support networks need to be improved. Currently workers build their own networks and sometimes it works and sometimes it does not. We are always adopting the most convenient thing. Mobile devices are just part of the package. Millennials connect using mobile methods, but in several different ways. Everyone is just trying to get the answers. In theory we have everything we need. We have all the right tools, even though new ones will continue to evolve. But we do not have the support mechanisms, people, training, contacts, etc.

Who do I call for "X"? We build our own networks and sometimes we get good information and sometimes we get bad information. When I have a question, how do I articulate it and how do I go get it resolved? This problem is exaggerated in the remote workplace. To get an answer the worker has to go to HR or IT support or procurement and is virtually all over the place trying to chase down an answer. We need to support people working remotely with strong support networks. This is necessary in face-to-face environments but critical in the remote workplace to make that person more effective and efficient.

Neal thinks there needs to be some sort of aggregation of contacts and technologies. Most organizations have too many technologies and everybody is using a different set of tools, and no one is sure what to use, when or how to respond. Some organizations use SMS (Short Message Service), others rely mostly on email, others use Microsoft Teams or Slack or Google. Some use them all. There needs to be a personal aggregate that helps people to navigate the arsenal of technologies that are available and provides them with the information and touchpoints they need. The only industry that operates like this is Finance and that is because they are so strictly regulated.

Neal gives a perfect example of his wife and daughter and friend asking why he did not respond to their SMS text for hours. He indicates it was because he was on his computer and not on his phone. The point is that more technologies is not necessarily better and can be frustrating and confusing. Most people have multiple emails, personal and business, tons of other collaboration software, and text messaging options, but there is nothing that is bringing it all together. This can make contact in the remote workplace confusing and frustrating. People miss things. He said, maybe a hologram of my mother stating "Neal, pay attention to this" would help!

We continue to create new channels of communication that are much more ubiquitous, but don't really think about the communications. We don't put parameters around it and in the remote workplace it takes time and effort just to sort through all the information that is continually coming at us. Neal said, the answer seems to be a single sign-on portal where when I wake up in the morning, I go to work, and I sign on (wherever I am) and everything I need is right there. That's where leadership comes in. Neal shares the example of customer support and multiple channels and limited execution. Customers can call for support, although it is sometimes difficult to talk with a human, they can email, or they can talk to a chatbot or a human on a chat app. Sometimes one of these methods is helpful and sometimes not. It depends on the importance leadership places on customer service.

With the COVID-19 crisis, Neal believes he should be able to go to one place to get the answers. Right now, he is faced with multiple emails, texts, posts, and on and on. People do not know what to pay attention to. Is the COVID-19 message from Human Resources the same as the one that came from the department manager? We have too many pieces of technology and no plan for communications.

The real issue is trust. Management does not trust people to work remotely. In a face-to-face environment, I can walk into your office and say, "I need this done" and you can say "That isn't part of my job description." Then I'll say "Yeah, but I know you can do it." In a remote environment management tends to keep workers in a box because it takes more effort to reach beyond that, which is the opposite of the idea that workers want to learn and grow, and that the organization should support them in that endeavor.

Security can work both ways. There is no question it is needed but sometimes VPNs (Virtual Private Networks) lock out ridiculous things and firewalls keep people from being able to do their jobs. Very few companies have trained workers on the requirements and legal aspects of the remote workplace. If IT has been trained, that is probably the only group that has been trained, and in most cases they have not been trained either.

Neal explained that his family life has been impacted by his working remotely, but he says their interactions are better. They respect each other's boundaries and keep business separate from their private lives. They key is respecting each other's privacy and scheduling and doing things together, like getting out for a walk in the afternoon. The dynamics are different when you work for someone else. You must determine what is OK and what is not OK. It's not a work-life balance, it's a work-life blend. The dynamics of work-life balance is in a different dimension when you work remotely. Business is changing and will continue to change to survive. We will have a new workforce and a new workforce standard. We are not going backward. Neal believes we are on the cusp of tremendous change in the business world.

Bottom line, on a scale of 1 to 4, 1 being I do not want to do this anymore and 4 I love it, Neal indicated he would be a 4. The benefits outweigh the challenges. The freedom, flexibility and independence offered are part of who he is, and he loves working from home #WFH! WOOT!

When I asked Neal six months later, in September 2020, what had changed, here is what he said: Initially my clients struggled to organize, attend and perform while sheltered in place but now they are finally moving forward, getting used to the technologies and beginning to get things done. On a personal basis, we are closer and talk more socially, not just about business. I miss going to the movies with my wife and getting out of the house. I miss going anywhere, just getting out and spending a day catching up with clients. We communicate differently. We don't save it up until we see each other, we share more instantly. Watching TV is far from comparable to sitting in a theater and having popcorn and not being interrupted by texts, phones and pings. This experience has broadened my exposure to new technologies and made me work harder to keep up with them. I don't like that decisions are being made more slowly and budgetary considerations are blocking progress, but I can see a shift in awareness. People are now beginning to see that working from home is possible, [and are] opening up to new possibilities, and technology in general.

When I interviewed David in early April 2020 he, **David** in contrast to Neal, did not like working from home. David said he would much rather be in the office. He is another seasoned independent consultant with lots of experience in technologies, but he does not embrace the working from home experience with the same vigor and enthusiasm that Neal does. David has been in the world of technology for decades. He is a seasoned executive and entrepreneur and sits on a lot of boards. He describes himself as very hands-on and an engineer who can read a balance sheet. He is currently acting as President for a well-established IT firm, the oldest in his state. Although most of his company has worked remotely for the last eight to ten years, he's a go to the office kind of guy.

Consisting mostly of programming and project management talent, his company has been relatively insulated from the remote worker paradigm shift that is taking place. Their people have always been remote workers. In doing climate surveys with the staff during the COVID-19 crisis, about 20% of the people said they do not want to work from home, they prefer to be on site because they like the interaction with clients and colleagues. Those folks that did typically work from home didn't work a standard 8 AM to 4 PM kind of job, they put in their eight hours somewhere between 7 AM and 8 PM. They enjoy the freedom of being able to go to the store or pick up the kids from school. With the COVID-19 forced remote workplace, they do not enjoy those same freedoms. For one thing, the kids are at home.

Over 45% of the workforce in David's firm hold visas. Rather than a "gig economy" or temporary positions and short-term commitments, he describes this workforce as a series of long-term commitments on a short-term basis, renewed over and over again. They work primarily with large companies, government agencies and big corporations. The companies like this arrangement because they can shut down the operation on short notice. The workers do not like it because it is highly stressful, and they are always worried about getting the next contract. Am I going to get extended? The workers want security. David's company pays for upgrading certifications and continuing education, and provides some sense of belonging and loyalty for workers. They provide benefits like insurance and some job security. They talk about career security instead of job security.

The impact of remote work on the wage structure has been a passthrough. Even if wages might be lower, there is still the cost of recruiting the remote worker, and talent management companies generally have no standards. Generally, small to midsize businesses do not attract the best talent. Depending on the industry, the workforce may vary in levels of education and length of employment. Because there is often a middle organization taking up to 4%, there is no long-term savings for the hiring company.

David is an up early and in the office kind of guy, even on the weekend. He is not married, has never been married, and has no children. He gets into the office by 5:30 AM and admits to being an unapologetic workaholic. Before the COVID-19 lockdown, meetings were usually face to face. He would go out to breakfast or meet in the office. Since the crisis, meetings are on Skype, Zoom or GoToMeeting. The number of meetings he attends has not decreased but the venue has changed. He still has several meetings every day.

When asked if the SMB (small to midsize businesses) were ready for the remote workplace, his response was "absolutely not." They were not ready to support people working from home with technology, systems, or access. They never embraced the approach. They never thought they would have to do it with their own staff. They literally had to have a gun to their head that was usually held by the employee saying, "we don't want to come in" or "we don't feel safe." Often, they had to borrow equipment where they could find it. One of David's clients is a large hotel casino that thought that by spreading the rumor that their air conditioning system had ultraviolet capabilities, and was killing the germs so the patrons had nothing to worry about, they could stay open. They shut down six days later and are still closed. They are genuinely concerned about reopening and the restrictions of social distancing.

The crisis has stressed the system, but really has not changed the way employers are looking at employment laws and compliance issues, at least not yet. David asked one of his leadership groups, "When did it go from a crisis on the other side of the world to a personal situation?" He got responses like, "When the sports season was cancelled," "When I was told to work from home," or "When the kids were no longer in school."

Extraordinarily, little of David's workforce uses mobile platforms. Although most of them have the equipment, their jobs are not conducive to working from the park or the local Starbucks. They are IT people, and they are sitting at their desk and looking at their device(s). They usually do not have an urgent need to respond. They are working on their projects. As producers of content, programmers, or project managers, they are evaluated for their productivity based on the number of completes. A higher level manager's performance is tied to the completes of those they are supervising and their ability to meet top-line or bottom-line expense controls and budgets. They do not experience many compatibility problems because they use all their own software. They use a VPN (Virtual Private Network) connection.

Bottom line, on a scale of 1 to 4, 1 being I do not want to do this anymore and 4 is I love it, David indicated he would be a 2. He likes going into the office, even though he admits that most of what he does could be done from anywhere. He gets phone calls at all hours of the day and night, but it really does not bother him because he does not have much of a personal life anyway. He plays a lot of roles. He is accessible from about 6 AM to about 9 PM. He does try to listen to his sister's advice and make appointments with himself for things like dinner engagements and other social activities. If David had to give advice to SMB owners, he would tell them to get ready for change

When I asked David six months later, this is what he said: Companies are continuing to downsize significantly and keep essential positions only. Domestic business travel is significantly reduced, and virtual communication is growing stronger and is more widely used. We have a virtual open-door policy on one video channel so clients can easily join in real time. I miss recreational activities, but nothing related to work. Most of our workers have been remote for years so the new normal looks exactly like the old. The competition is increasing, and more companies are going remote, which makes us more creative and competitive. I have learned to love working from home, now it would be a 4!

Stan   When I interviewed Stan in early April 2020, he was somewhere in the middle. Stan works for the public sector, local county government. He sits on the board of a county Chamber of Commerce that is one of the largest in the state. He is exposed to all varieties of business, large and small. With the advent of COVID-19, the Chamber was actively involved with selling gift cards for local businesses with the idea of trying to help them stay alive during the shutdown. Everyone is working from home and they have adjusted as much as is possible.

The Chamber has transitioned to virtual networking events, which do not tend to be as popular as the face-to-face ones. The run more than a dozen of these each month. One in particular, "joke night," seems to be extremely popular during these trying times with about 100 people showing up where they usually get about 20. Again, this shows how desperate people are for connection and trying to keep a sense of humor and figure out what is going on during the COVID-19 lockdown. Stan has seen this same reaction again and again.

Leadership made a huge difference in the move to the online and virtual workplace. The real challenge has been in the diversity of membership. Some businesses adjusted well, and others Stan fears will not adjust at all. There will be a high toll for the inability to move to the new remote workplace. Some businesses will just not make it. There are also some legal issues with giving advice. Although the Chamber has been passing on only official information, some businesses are making recommendations that they will own, and with that comes liability. If they advise people not to go into the office and the business folds because of that, it creates problems. People are in survival mode and not really looking beyond the day to day. Stan's own feeling is that when this passes and business reacclimates, it is going to be an entirely different world. Department stores will not be the same, and many office buildings will be vacant.

Stan also has a practice as a national consultant. Under different circumstances he would go out to the client's office and work in their conference room or rent a hotel conference room nearby. In Stan's opinion the biggest challenge to working from home is the different needs of different businesses both by size and by industry.

He sees companies developing fluid schedules and not necessarily working from 9 to 5. He added regular walking and exercise to his daily routine. His biggest challenge is educating his clients that the work that he does can be done virtually because traditionally it is done face to face. It is a mind-shift. The work can be done online, it is just a question of changing clients' perspectives.

Stan indicated that on a scale of 1 to 4, 1 being I do not want to do this anymore and 4 I love it, he would be a 3. He enjoys the face-to-face connections and that is why he chose the business that he is in, but he likes the convenience and admits that working from home works pretty well. He would rather work from home 100% than have to be in the office 100%. He prefers the blend, the mix; a little of each would give him the best of both worlds. He and his wife are both currently working from home, but that is really no problem because they have plenty of room. Each person has their own space and they can shut the door to their offices and have complete privacy, more or less.

Moving forward, the advice he would give business is to make sure they have the right platforms, systems, and connectivity. He has experienced an exceedingly difficult time with VPN, and he has tried a few different varieties. None of them have delivered what he had hoped for. The VPNs slow his system down and limit access. He thinks the choice is poor connectivity or no VPN. From a security standpoint he is encrypted and more secure but the connectivity and access leaves something to be desired. One option was so bad, he walked away from a full year contract, fully paid, and tried another option, which was not that much better. Stan needs the security because of the kind of information he deals with for his clients.

Stan's favorite communication tools are the synchronous video platforms. He has 8 to 10 meetings a week and uses them for personal, business, and community-related meetings. He had a virtual Passover seder dinner and loved it! They had family from Pennsylvania, Chicago, Massachusetts, and Maryland all in attendance. He finds video conferencing easy and effortless. It is just a matter of sending a link and communicating. He finds video conferencing makes the focus and concentration much more direct.

Coming out of this crisis, Stan feels we are going to enter a new world. No one misses the hour-and-a-half commute. The new normal will be vastly different. The new workplace will take a while to unfold. Offices will be different, technological infrastructure and physical infrastructure will change. Businesses will have to take technology more seriously and access will need to be more secure and universal. Business will be leaner, and AI (Artificial Intelligence) will really take off. He sees the demand for office buildings changing greatly. In Stan's words, "you might need a new dentist office, but you won't need a new office for engineers." He also is taking online courses and thinks that the ability to keep your skills up to date and learn online is a trend that will really take off.

When I asked Stan six months later, this is what he said: We have had to reinvent ourselves and we are still in that process. I am marketing for the first time, alerting clients to new formats, and find there is a greater acceptance of virtual communication since traditional means of conducting business has been compromised. The big question is are clients still willing to engage with the old services in a new format? Daily activities like grocery shopping are more stressful and difficult and have to be planned. I have felt the full impact of the pandemic and am still adjusting to the changes. I would still be a 3. I like working from home, but I miss the people-to-people connections.

When I interviewed Pete who is Vice President of Human Resources, in early April 2020, he said he thinks they have done the best they could have under the circumstances. He heads up a staff of four people, three in California and one in Ohio. His company had nothing on the cloud. No, we were not ready for this at all, he said. We are a family owned, old-school printing company and have been around for almost 40 years. The business is printing, packaging, mail, and fulfillment. The company is kind of a one-stop shop for business communication solutions. They are considered an essential business and were allowed to remain open. They do a fair amount of business with pharmaceuticals and medical companies.

Pete sees working from home as a major adjustment. He likes working from home but thinks jobs in Human Resources and some individuals in particular really require a face-to-face environment. He thinks if working from home is to be a long-term solution, it will take some thought and reengineering for it to be as productive and effective as possible. It is not for everyone and it's not for every position. He has experience in the remote workplace from a prior life where he was a consultant, but this business is a vastly different environment. About 58% of the workforce is production oriented. There are a lot of positions that just cannot be done remotely. They have huge Heidelberg printing presses, and they require face-to-face operations. Mostly, Pete admits it is a question of mindset. He sees marketing, sales, human resources, IT, accounting, and finance as all requiring some face-to-face contact. He does admit that the general and accounting side of the business has a better chance at success in the remote workplace than the actual production people.

Chapter 4

There's No and Then There's Hell No!

Pete

Production is a "Hell no!" They really cannot work from home.

They were not ready for this. They did not have the equipment. Not everyone had a laptop. Many people still had tower desktop computers. He finds employee relations incredibly challenging in the remote world. He finds that conversations are skewed when delivered via email. The tone, the expressions and the meaning can easily be distorted. He finds it difficult to have strategic conversations and brainstorming session online. Meetings are all right but insightful work, not so much. He is used to the whiteboard and storyboarding and everyone giving input. He finds the sense of comradery, a shared mindset, is different online. He misses the comradery of walking down the hall and having a conversation. According to Pete, picking up the phone is an extra step some people will not take. Walking down the hall is more natural, easier. Email has a delay in terms of send and receive, and because you need to wait, it is not as effective as a face-to-face conversation. This situation was thrust upon the company and there really was no plan for working remotely. If working remotely is a long-term proposition, Pete feels that a little more thought needs to go into to it to make it effective for everyone.

Pete's plan so far has been to be as preemptive as possible, but so far the company has been mostly reactive. He tries to initiate conversation and be proactive. Pete used the example of a triangle with the tactical part of the operations at the bottom, operations in the middle and strategic at the top. He tries to think strategically but feels that the company has been stuck in operations since moving to the remote workplace. His group in HR is in charge of relating information about the Coronavirus from the CDC and making sure that the information is distributed, posted, and in compliance with the California state regulations for essential businesses, since they have remained open. They have people who have been laid off, lots of unemployment claims, and modified work schedules. He feels like he is on a hamster wheel and is just trying to stay ahead of the situation. He is working hard to make sure he complies with employment law in California and Ohio. He consults legal counsel often but still feels like it is tough to stay ahead of the situation. There are people working from home, people who must come in and people who have been let go.

Most of the company's communications are done with email. He reports to one of the owners. In the beginning, they spoke at least twice a day. Six weeks into it, that has changed, and he now just regularly communicates with his team. He checks in with them once a day, in the afternoon. Payroll has also been interesting. They applied and received the payroll protection loan, but now are unsure how they will apply it. According to Pete it took a lot of data scrubbing and work to get the information together. In the middle of this crisis, they had their plant manager in Ohio die suddenly, which left that location without leadership at exactly the wrong time. It was truly a perfect storm.

It's settling down a little about seven weeks in to COVID-19, but so far it has been mostly crisis management. The tools they are using like Zoom and Microsoft Teams are also new to the organization. They were not using them before the lockdown. Workers were not used to communicating this way and had to learn the tools on top of everything else. IT had to set up the tools, the access, VPN, and support this move, quickly. IT and HR have been overwhelmed. They had to set a lot of people up in systems where they did not have access before.

When I asked Pete whether the company was ready to work from home, his response was, "There's no and then there's hell no." With the COVID-19 crisis, he does think the company has tried to support anyone who could work from home to make it work. In normal times, he thinks there would have been much more of a resistance to remote work. The mindset is one that if you work from home, you are not really working, you're goofing around. There is a lack of trust. All three owners are brothers and have only ever worked for this company.

Pete was concerned about workers' compensation claims, and had questions like, if a worker got injured in their home, do they have their own insurance? Moving forward, he is sure the option to work from home will be totally dependent on the job position and the person. He is concerned about ergonomics, OSHA, and other labor issues as well. It is apparent this business has had its share of legal engagements over employee claims.

Pete also finds a big difference between the generations. In general, he finds the younger people (20s and 30s) to be more flexible than those that are older (50s and 60s). He finds that the level of trust depends on the individual, how long they have been with the company and the person's maturity. He is concerned that the older folks may not be as tech savvy and might have a difficult adjustment to make to work from home. On the other hand, young people are not necessarily more or less trustworthy than older folks.

Pete admits that continuing the remote workplace beyond the immediate future would require a makeover of the organizational structure. They are used to a face-to-face environment and structurally are not prepared for the virtual workplace. Most of their Learning and Development is done in a show and tell kind of setting, with individual managers coming off the production lines to demonstrate. There are a lot of logistic issues ranging from space to equipment. He admits the company is more old school with their information systems being housed on site behind a firewall. Authentication, dual sign on, and other more modern techniques are out of their wheelhouse. They are not a cloud-based company and really had no plans to move in that direction. They do not have a portal and home is a quite different online environment than on site. It is really VPN access to a few network drives and email. They also do not have an intranet.

At the bottom of all this, there is still an issue of trust. If the bosses feel comfortable with the individual, like Pete, who has been with the company for eight years, and has shown loyalty and dedication, there is a higher level of trust. If the individual is newer or there are difficulties with the work environment at home, there is less trust. One of Pete's employees has a home situation where there are two spouses and three children, all being schooled from home, sharing a small apartment in the San Francisco Bay area. Two other team members are younger, in their twenties, and share a ridiculously small apartment because of the expensive rent, and are now both working from the kitchen table. There are issues with noise and privacy and babysitting. Another issue is time management and that really depends on the person's ability to manage themselves. Pete mentions that often these same issues with time management showed themselves in the face-to-face workplace but have been magnified with people working remotely.

On a scale of 1 to 4, 1 being I do not want to do this anymore and 4 I love it, he would be a 3. Pete really likes working from home but considers himself an extrovert and likes face-to-face contact. To work from home full time would require some planning and reengineering of his job role. His wife works from home three days a week and has for years. He also has a daughter, a sophomore in college who is now studying from home, and another older daughter, and everyone is using the same internet connection which really can strain the bandwidth with everyone on synchronous platforms simultaneously. They have multiple hubs, but it is still a strain on the systems.

It is also a strain on relationships. His wife told him he is loud, and he talks all day long, which he fully admits to and describes it as the nature of his position, which is Vice President of Human Resources. He is online all day long, answering questions and interacting with people's problems and issues. It is not easy to share the same physical space with anyone. He does not miss the forty-five-minute commute each way, each day, at all. He appreciates being able to sleep in a bit more and get up and start working without the traffic and hassles. Some of the people he works with do two-hour commutes. When he first started working remotely, he felt that he was always on. He could not find the off button and was experiencing stress and burnout. He admits to taking calls at dinnertime from owners because of expectations and fear of turning things off. This is common in the virtual workplace depending on management, expectations, and trust levels. Pete does think he works more in the remote environment because of the 24/7 connectivity and of course the crisis mode of COVID-19. He equates it to working for a startup, with longer hours, both earlier and later. He is doing his best to establish a routine, including exercise three days a week, and that is helping to stabilize his new work environment.

His suggestion for moving forward in the remote environment is to create a set of deliverables and clear expectations for employee performance. Developing a way to measure productivity, a consistent communication schedule and hiring the right people are important. He strongly feels not everyone is cut out for the remote workplace. He also feels that it is not for every position, operations or management. If people are going to work from home, they need an environment that is suitable and sustainable. Also, they need clear expectations and the ability to set boundaries. He finds the remote workplace blurs boundaries.

When I asked Pete six months later, this is what he said: Working from home can work for many roles that at one time we thought were impossible. We are working on establishing new guidelines, telecommuting policies, proper ergonomic set-up and applicable reimbursement for expenses. Managers are trying to develop expectations tied to results, metrics and deliverables, and to communicate these. The manager's mindset is shifting from "checking up to checking in" on their staff. Managers need to learn to trust their employees and know that they are working productively and efficiently, which is another reason we need to develop the metrics. Working from home is not as easy as going next door to talk with my staff. There is more time spent on communications but there are less interruptions. The mindset of the owners is shifting, and they now support working from home. Working from home is a work in progress. I don't think it is as efficient as when I'm in the office, but I am redefining it, and it is improving, he says. What will happen next is hugely unknown. A lot of it depends on the company's revenue. If revenue picks up and increases, then we will hire more staff. Right now, the company is in a holding pattern and managing "must haves." Right now, we are doing more with less. We need to improve our means, mode and style of communications. This is key. #WFH will be part of our future.

Finance is probably one of the most tightly regulated industries in the United States. The SEC (The U.S. Securities and Exchange Commission) controls access, interactions and sharing information: No cell phones at your desk and no doing business from your friend's house in the Hamptons. I spoke with Brad in early April 2020. He is a Vice President at a Wall Street firm that is considered a broker dealer that trades securities, bonds, loans, and equities, and they buy and sell to investors. It is all about market exposure, visibility, and perceived value. Brad did not go home right away. He held off because he really likes being on the trading floor. He likes the little conversations and the informal interactions that make Wall Street what it is. It is an old-school atmosphere where people still shout about deals and the energy is intense and continuous.

Working from home, he misses his connections. He has a phone turret that they call the "hoot" which connects everyone. It is constant information; he can hear what the traders are trading, and it is a lifeline to everyone in the firm. From a technology and equipment standpoint, the firm has a remote portal interface that works well. Once he signs onto the system, it is just like being in the office, but he could be anywhere. Brad was a little concerned about the systems, accessibility, and communications, but in his opinion that is all working out well. Remote access is a little slower, about 10%. Everything takes just a little bit longer than in the office.

Before COVID-19, he had rarely worked from home. It is just not what Wall Street executives do. His firm did not provide any equipment—no laptop, no internet, no monitors. Setting up the home

Chapter 5

Wall Street Never Really Closed

Brad

environment was his responsibility. Several firms he refers to did not close their offices because they just did not have enough laptops to go around. For him, no one offered anything and no one checked to see if he was functioning online. The firm has been sending out regulatory information—because of the extremely strict regulations in the industry, there is a huge regulatory burden working from home. He really feels like the firms that did send people home waited too long. They did not act responsibly.

The good news is that his firm's systems and security are set up so that once he logs into the portal, it is just like being at the office. He is working on the same interface, systems, and drives. He logs in the same way and feels like he is on his work computer. He has dual encryption and two factor authentications. He goes to a website, logs in and then it rings his phone and asks him "Is this you?" He approves the connection, and then logs in again. Communication is still a challenge. The physical space is challenging, and the lack of equipment is difficult. At home he has one monitor; in the office he had four. He feels he is less efficient.

Communications is conducted using a program call Bloomberg Chat. It is how Wall Street communicates. It's like Slack or Microsoft Teams but it is for the Street. Brad has a personal cell phone, but the firm did not supply one. Typically, in the office, he is not allowed to be on his cell phone at his desk. Because of compliance regulations, they actively monitor this. They put in strict regulations about it and many other things. Since going remote, they have created a whole new level of protocol because everyone is using their cell phones. The regulation says if you talk to anyone on your cell phone, you need to write down what you said and who you talked to. The SEC has never had to deal with working from home before. Most of these guidelines were written for a face-to-face office environment. In the office, they monitor every link very closely, even access to social media like LinkedIn, but at home things are different. The compliance team at the firm sends out a lot of emails to avoid liability issues, but in reality it is only so effective. They really cannot monitor location and client connections the way they do face-to-face. The SEC requires that his communications be monitored and logged. The fact that he is on a home computer and his personal cell phone is unique to this situation and a regulatory challenge. Navigating the regulatory issues and making decisions out of the office puts the responsibility on the individual.

Daily, other than the commute, Brad's schedule is about the same. He starts the day with a group call at 7:30 AM. The rest of the day, he is stuck in front of a computer. In the office he would be going out to lunch or going to a meeting. Now he stays connected because if someone needs to connect with Brad, he needs to be there. The day winds down around 5 PM and he no longer feels like he is glued to the screen. He feels his days are longer and everyone he knows feels the same way. They are working more and spending more time doing it. Everyone is glued to their computers all day, every day. The only saving grace is that they are market-based and the market closes at 4, so things can wind down by around 5 PM.

In its own way, he feels like Wall Street was ready for the remote workplace. Because they were already so strictly regulated by the SEC, the security and protocol for remote work was in place. Because a lot of people work between branch offices and the main office in New York, people working from different locations was not new to them. They use Bloomberg Anywhere which has its own two factor identification and is fingerprint verified, and email is also verified with a thumbprint. He logs into Microsoft Teams and the company email, but nothing lives on his phone. No Zoom, no video chats, no synchronous connections.

The performance expectations are not clear, but they were not clear in the office either. Just do your job and that is it. It is the way Wall Street operates. Some of the leadership sent people to branch locations, rather than sending people home. They felt more comfortable with Connecticut people going to the Connecticut office and New Jersey people going into that branch. They did not feel comfortable just sending people home to work . A lot of people are still going into the offices in New York and have been through the whole pandemic. Many older, seasoned traders just do not feel comfortable doing business any other way and the firm has remained open. The leadership never told people what to do, they left it up to the individual. If they wanted to work from home they could, but they kept the office open for those who wanted that. Brad feels that across Wall Street some firms have shut down, but some have never even really considered it. People were still going into the office because that was the environment where they felt comfortable working. For the most part, he feels the Finance industry has tried to comply with the #WFH orders of the governor and wants people to be safe through the Coronavirus pandemic. Generally, San Francisco, Los Angeles, Chicago, and London all told people to work from home.

On a scale of 1 to 4, 1 being I do not want to do this anymore and 4 I love it, he would be a 2.75 or a 3. He would love to have the option of selecting times when he could work from home, but until COVID-19 sent people home, working from home always had a stigma attached to it. It is an issue of trust. There was an assumption that if you said you were working from home you were really goofing off. People have gotten fired over this issue. There is that old-school belief that someone must be physically in the office to man the ship and if you are really at work, you are really in the office where everyone can see you. Brad also admitted that he likes the face-to-face office environment. It is also what he is accustomed to. He has discovered that working from home has some benefits and if attitudes towards #WFH change, he would love to have that option because it cuts out the commute.

Brad finds it harder to squeeze in extracurricular activities than he did when he was in the office. He stays online a little longer, hangs around the desk a little more. Brad finds it more difficult to pull himself out of the apartment and make it to the gym to go do his workout. This is intensified because it is New York, and initially everything officially was closed for COVID-19. New York was the epicenter of the pandemic early on. He does like the personal space as compared to the office and trading floor where even receiving a phone call is prohibited. He likes the freedom and flexibility in the work from home environment. He thinks the line between work and personal life has blurred, not blended, and that has both positive and negatives.

Moving forward, if he were going to continue to work from home, he would set up more equipment, monitors and a turret. Brad would like some help with setting up his remote workplace, so that he is not responsible for the whole thing. Someone from IT at the firm might set up things like the docking station and connectivity. If you are working for a company, that company needs to help you create a workspace that is workable. Brad also feels there could be more emphasis on strategy and planning, which has been lost during quarantine. People log into calls and do their jobs, but he misses the little conversations that happen between colleagues. He misses the watercooler talk and feels like those conversations are invaluable to understanding where the firm is headed and what is coming down the pike. Rumors of people being let go because of a downturn in the market and the lack of communication can be disconcerting.

His friend, who is a programmer for Wall Street, loves working from home. He dreads going back to an open office space. He loves being able to focus and get the work done. Brad admits that for him, it is easier to focus at home too. Trading floors of Wall Street remain notorious for constant conversation, yelling and excitement and not for quiet concentration. He says he can focus and if he needs a quiet moment to concentrate, he can get one. He is on the research side of things and his job is much different than a trader. He is required to think about complex capital structures and industries and make inferences and connections. The quiet and peace he experiences being a single guy alone in his apartment makes working from home something he really appreciates. Wall Street is in limbo and it may take years before the impact of COVID-19 plays out. It will be difficult if not impossible to tell if the impact on the Street is related to working from home or the economic influence of the actions taken because of the pandemic.

When I asked Brad six months later, this is what he said: I'm working way harder and there are fewer ways to mess around. It can get incredibly stressful when there is a lot of action or need. It's a little harder to get things done. It's easier to sit down for three minutes, but overall it is more efficient use of my time. A lot less gets written down or printed out than in the office. I've found it a little difficult to have the sidebar conversations and quick catch ups that make work interesting and colorful. It is also harder to meet new clients, which might be related to the pandemic as much as working from home. I am getting to the point that I really want to meet up with more friends and clients and exchange ideas. Those that were harder to get a hold of are now easier and those that were easier are now harder to reach. I miss restaurants and casual meetings the most. The company has backed us 100% and we are allowed to work from home indefinitely, but I am not sure what that really means. Working from home carries way less stigma and is becoming the normal way to work. I appreciate the flexibility and that part is wonderful. Also I find getting in touch with people who are further away and terribly busy is easier than before. I am a 3.25 now. I have grown to appreciate #WFH a little more but still miss my people.

"Emergency Remote Teaching" is not good online learning. The two are quite different. When COVID-19 hit Higher Education, what they went with was the former not the later. Most of Higher Education was in no way ready to go online. In fact, they had been fighting it for decades. When I interviewed Sarah in early April 2020, she had been an Assistant Dean of Online Learning for a prominent university for years. She typically oversees relationships with an OPM (Online Program Management) organization, trains faculty and does whatever it takes to keep the online programs in her school up and running. The university hired a third party and paid dearly over an extended period because they did not want to invest in online internally. Like many schools, they thought this was a fad and it would pass. With the COVID crisis she was asked to work with many additional faculty to get their face-to-face courses online in a week.

Sarah has been working from home for three years. She lives in a lovely little town and has an eight-year-old son. She is a single mom. Initially, she struggled with feeling guilty for being able to work from home and felt like she needed to work more. Having leadership that supported her helped tremendously. Now, she feels like she has a good schedule and pace and is extremely comfortable working remotely. However, her new leadership does not share that view.

She thinks the work-life balance is the most difficult aspect of working from home because the actual physical environment causes the line to be blurred. Having an eight-year-old at home all day because of the COVID-19 quarantine only makes it more difficult. She now has three full time jobs:

Chapter 6

Higher Ed Goes Emergency Remote

Sarah

Assistant Dean, Mom and second grade teacher. What her son is doing is homeschooling, not online learning. She is given a list of assignments and activities and they are on their own to get it done and hand it in at the end of the week. She tries to schedule all her meetings in the morning because her son is better at working independently then; after lunch his concentration is not as strong.

Typically, before COVID, she managed a staff of three and did faculty training and met with her staff. Every Wednesday morning they had a team meeting. Before COVID she had two to four meetings a day, but four was rare; since COVID she is averaging six to eight meetings a day. She is in meetings online all day, every day, for six to eight hours. She thinks it is a reaction from leadership that they are truly uncomfortable with remote work. To get the faculty online she created trainings and scheduled office hours on an online scheduling platform, where they can easily book an appointment with her. She tried extremely hard to stick to that schedule and not react to the requests of faculty for help "right now." Trying to get all the faculty acclimated and online has extended the day considerably. She used to work basically nine to four; now it more like eight to eight, at least. Her university often imposes their desire to please others and meet their wants and needs on her. Her struggle to keep a consistent schedule is difficult because she doesn't get their support. There is a general lack of boundaries around the workday. She gets texts and phone calls late at night from her boss who wants something before an early morning meeting the next day. She understands that this comes from a sense of panic and an attempt to control what is generally out of control.

Sarah feels that she and her team were ready for the remote workplace. She made sure her team had laptops and webcams from the time they started as well as secure remote access and connections. The overall organization was not ready. It is not the school's policy to give everyone a laptop. Just from a hardware perspective, the organization was not ready to go remote. People did not have the internet connections they needed either. Some of the staff is older and lacks the skills, and some of the systems are housed locally and not available for remote access.

Before the COVID situation, the leadership required her to come to the office one day a week for "optics," which was ridiculous. Her boss was quite hypocritical, on one hand bragging that they had remote workers and on the other hand making her drive into the office to be "seen." Now with the COVID pandemic, Sarah is a poster child for how you can work from home and still be productive and contribute. Everyone is coming to her asking for tips and tricks on how to be successful in this new environment. They want to know how she manages her team, her day and her work-life balance. Prior to the lockdown, the organization in general was very averse to remote work. It was a hiring issue or Human Resources problem and in areas like IT this caused turnover issues, and they could not hire and keep good people. The mental roadblock was based on fear that if we do this for one group, we will need to do it for everyone. Pre-COVID they were not ready to take that leap. Again, it comes back to ignorance and leadership not really understanding the technologies and what they have to offer the workplace. Sarah is sure that COVID was a wake-up call and policy will be impacted.

In the middle of our interview, her eight-year-old son came into the room, terribly upset because his second-grade teacher did not call on him during a Zoom "show and tell." Not only was Higher Education unprepared for this, K-12 basically ground to a halt. More on this in the next chapter, but putting education online requires more than just sticking a Chromebook in a kid's hands.

There are a lot of issues with working from home that this #WFH situation has brought to light. Local labor laws are only one of them. Many industries are governed by federal laws that require compliance and in education FERPA (Family Education Rights and Privacy Act) is one of them. FERPA is a federal law that protects the privacy of student educational records. The law applies to all institutions that receive any kind of federal funding from the U.S. Department of Education. Sarah does have a contract with HR that states the requirements for her working remotely. She had to answer questions like do you have a separate home office, does it have windows, do you have a fire extinguisher in the house? She uses her own printer and pays for her own ink. She has received no training on FERPA. Because she is technically savvy, she does try to make faculty aware that recording and sharing your class meeting on social media is not a good idea. The institution really has not addressed any of these kinds of issues. They do have some policies in place in the student code of conduct but visibility and privacy in the remote environment are mostly not addressed.

Using Microsoft Teams has really helped Sarah with team collaboration in the remote work environment. They use it for mobile communications and chat. It also helps to segregate personal and work communications. They do not SMS text on personal numbers because they try to keep all the communications on Teams. Pre-COVID, they had the technology, but it was difficult to get people to use Teams. Post-COVID, things have changed. She measures productivity by "are you getting it done," not by hours or time online. Sarah has faith in her staff and encourages innovation and contribution. It's important for her to see her team motivated and she encourages new ideas and getting results.

Her team and most of the people she works with have the hardware and software they need to work remotely. The university has done a good job of providing equipment, hardware, software, and connection. What Sarah does find is that the normal glitches that everyone experiences using technologies cause panic in people who are not used to communicating in this manner. It has been especially challenging with faculty. The challenge is heightened when they adopt new technologies and change software platforms. The government banned one synchronous platform and encouraged the use of another, which is inside the LMS (Learning Management System), and this was new uncharted territory. Pushback and negativity can spiral into panic. The only real security issues they have faced so far is with government employees. She does get pushback from purchasing about buying new software applications, which are very inexpensive. Sarah credits this to a genuine lack of understanding by administration on why these tools are helpful and why Apple iOS (iPhone Operating System) tools are often different than Microsoft Windows applications. The VPN is required for library access but not really anything else. Most of the university is still on local drives and is not cloud based. Because the online classes are facilitated by OPMs (Online Program Management), some are on a local version of Blackboard and some cloud based, there are a host of different connection, security and access issues. One of the challenges is consistency. Every school— there are five different ones within their university— and group can pretty much use whatever they want and do whatever they want to do. They all have different LMSs, different expectations and different policies.

On a scale of 1 to 4, 1 being I do not want to do this anymore and 4 I love it, she would be a 3.5. Because she manages a team, she values some personal contact and face-to-face engagement. Working virtually allows her to have a life. She is a single mom, and it gives her the opportunity to live where she does and still have this job. She appreciated working from home prior to COVID-19. #WFH allowed her to get her son on the bus every day and get him off the bus after school. It has also had a big impact on her health. She no longer needs to drive two and a half to three hours or more every day, so she has time for the gym and to teach yoga. She did get pushback from her supervisor because he wanted to work from home more often and wanted one of her team members to always be in the office. She gave him a flat out no way and threatened to leave the organization if he required her to be in the office two to three days a week. Again, it is a matter of trust, not on her supervisor's part but a concern of his boss's.

Moving forward, Sarah thinks it is critical that the remote workplace and the ability to be productive and successful in it be part of the hiring decision. She thinks the skillset required for working from home needs to be a consideration in almost every position. Everyone needs the ability to adapt technologically and understand the impact of schedules. More meetings are not better. There needs to be a level of trust in your staff. Productivity goes down, you waste time, and you get less done when there is a lack of trust.

Sarah explained that the university moved the AV (Audio Visual) team to Learning Support and made them remote workers because they had no need for AV when everyone went online. They were able to do this because the team was talented and technically savvy and able to adapt. She can see the benefit of a more centralized approach to working online. Because each school, and in some cases each department, at this university operates in siloed environment, the decisions are autonomous, and this can lead to problems. They do have a new president who is creating a new strategic plan with more collaboration than there was in the past. The centralized training tends to be broad and general; it does not currently meet the needs of individual faculty and staff. Without a centralized approach to the interface, to scheduling, to access, etc., working and learning online can be confusing. It is easy to waste a lot of time and get frustrated, and it can create a high level of anxiety in the learners and extra stress on the faculty and staff. Sarah thinks the biggest challenge is being open to change and learning new ways of doing things.

When I asked Sarah six months later, this is what she said: I did not talk to Sarah six months later. She never responded to my emails or calls. I suspect she was still terribly busy being an Assistant Dean, mom and homeschool teacher.

Will   I interviewed Will in early April 2020. He works with a cohort of about 80 Higher Education students in the process of obtaining their associate's or bachelor's degrees. Most of these students are working adults. The average age of these learners is about twenty-five. Most of them have some college behind them and are trying to finish a degree. He is an advisor, academic counselor, coach and trusted student success resource. Normally, he works in a student center in downtown Boston. Since COVID-19, everything has migrated online via text, email and Google. He shares a small apartment in Cambridge with his partner and their dog. His company went remote for a few days, which became a few weeks and turned into many months. Half of what they do was already online, so they were in a better position than most to be able to handle moving to the remote workplace. They use the phone, emails and Google Hangouts for most of their normal academic support activities. They had some digital momentum going.

As a coach and counselor, Will finds that conversations are different online; there is a different dynamic and different expectations evolve. He had to redevelop the rapport he has with his students. Because of the diversity of these learners, some coming from lower income populations, they might not be as familiar with digital connection and computers as others in their age group. With most of these learners he has been able to reestablish the connection, but some have disappeared entirely. He no longer connects with some and others have gone missing.

Will is comfortable working at home but it took some adjustment. His company went remote when the governor issued the stay at home quarantine. Before that, his company really hadn't thought of it. They thought the students were dependent on the space as a place to come for help, so they tried to stay open as long as possible. At first, he was excited to be at home and thought of it more like a vacation. But that didn't last more than a few days. His partner works from home all the time and he found that helpful. He more or less adopted her schedule. He thinks there is an ebb and flow to structuring the day and the term. Every day and every week have their challenges.

Student need dictates his focus. Some adult learners need more support than others. His students fall into one of three camps: they are self-sufficient and have a dedicated workspace at home and the equipment they need, those who are very dependent on the student center to get their work done, and those who are a mixed bag, they have the equipment, or some of it, but they still need a lot of support. How he supports each of these learners is a bit different in a remote environment.

Will is re-learning his job. There is a lot going on; process and procedures are changing. By default, these students enter their academic world through a portal. But there really wasn't a plan on how to communicate so he bounced around a bit between platforms and apps, and still does. Communications developed organically. Most of these learners are familiar with Google Documents, Hangouts, and Drive. This was covered in their onboarding.

His company has its own portal interface for financial aid, scheduling, and student information.

The work the students do is fed from their LMS into Microsoft Power BI and Will's company receives real time reporting on student activities and behavior. It's an incredible data stream. It's way too much really, he says. With seventy students the amount of data is overwhelming. Even consolidated into Excel spreadsheets, it can be dense. Will uses his private internet but has a work phone.

His biggest challenge is meeting his students where they are. Many of them have been laid off, are delinquent with rent, and have childcare issues. Many don't have food. School has taken a back seat out of necessity. They are anxious, uncertain and have to constantly readjust to new circumstances. Reaching out and communicating is key. He does cold calls and just tries to catch up. Some are more resilient; some not so much.

His hours are from 10 AM to 6 PM, more or less. He does the ten-step commute to the dining room table and gets started. He and his partner take breaks now and then and take time off for lunch. It's a pretty regular schedule. He works more now that he's home but he has more room to be in the zone and doesn't miss the commute at all. His company was pretty well equipped and ready. Half of what they did regularly was already online because these learners attend an online university. There really was no plan or official remote work agreement. HR is a bit behind in this area. They pivoted when COVID-19 sent everyone home and are "freestyling" in Will's words.

Students can connect to him anytime. He gets less emails now, but more phone calls and more texts. The number of meetings has also gone up. He has a team meeting daily. The meetings are small, usually five or six people. The technology has worked fairly well. His company really hasn't addressed any kind of remote compliance training. They do a lot of text messaging on group threads. With four student coaches on a team, there could be hundreds of texts going on in real time. It's very annoying but it works. It really helps student performance. Personally, he has to set his schedule and know when to turn it off.

On a scale of 1 to 4, 1 being I do not want to do this anymore and 4 I love it, Will would be a 3.2. If the option to work remotely wasn't because of COVID-19, he says it would be even higher. He likes the impact it has had on his private life and he thinks he has more free time. He gets to take a break when he needs one and goes with the flow. He works for a company that has a common business vision. They know what needs to be done and they communicate and do it. Clear expectations and a high level of trust are apparent. Everyone knows where "true north" is and that's where they are headed. He finds working from home more flexible and thinks it saves his energy.

To improve the remote working experience, he would suggest a more official schedule and some suggested expectations. Everyone has figured it out on their own, but his comfort level would increase if he knew, and everyone else knew, what the remote workday was supposed to look like and that they were meeting those expectations. Because the environment is so mixed between private life and business demands, he would like to know that he can have a private life and shut work off. Because of COVID, everything has been so crazy. Every day he is learning, and things are constantly changing.

When I asked Will six months later, this is what he said: At this point, the concept of "work-life balance" almost seems erroneous. Not having to commute to a workplace and stay there for eight hours has freed up a lot of mental bandwidth for me, and I actually find myself being far more productive and inclined to work longer, more focused hours. I would be totally okay with things not returning to normal or moving forward with a remote/in office hybrid. The new landscape of working from home has produced more benefits than problems. For Will, the loss of in-person contact with teammates and clients is by far the greatest opportunity cost to remote work. He said, I really do miss the human-to-human element of the office, and for this reason I would be in favor of a hybrid work model going forward. A couple days a week in the office might be the perfect solution.

My company has been incredibly supportive though all of this and has done an exceptionally good job of prioritizing employee needs, Will said. Employees have essentially been given an open canvas to design their work schedule around their lives, particularly employees with young kids at home, of which we have many. We have proceeded with the attitude of "do whatever you need to do as long as the work gets done." I think on the whole people have been happy with this. What I miss most definitely is being out in the world, amongst strangers, having the option to go to restaurants/bars, not having to worry about masks.

At least through the end of the year I will be working from home mostly, though I will be in the office twice a week, voluntarily. So much of what I do is already online/over the phone, [so] the adjustment to the new situation was pretty easy. I think long-term this will really benefit us, as it has forced us to step up our game with respect to student support. Not having our office open for student use was a big loss, and we have since become much more effective in our remote support. So far, this seems to have made many of us a lot better at our jobs. I would be a 4 now. I really like working from home and I think it has made me better at my job.

Chapter 7

K-12 Education Stops or Mostly

Jennifer

When I interviewed Jennifer in early April 2020, she said, "I am at the beach in New Jersey. It is not that I don't want to teach remotely, it is that I really can't." Jenifer teaches ninth and tenth grade English at an inner-city school. The neighborhood is much like the Bronx. She has many students who are ESL (English as a Second Language) Learners who need additional support. The reason she went into to teaching as a profession is because in her words "it feeds my inner extrovert." She enjoys the social interactions of the classroom and so do her students. They connect with her and that is what motivates them to learn. The students feed off her energy and give her energy. She chose education because of the connections and sees it as a profession all about humans, not about technologies. Although she admits she needs some private time to plan lessons and grade or write papers, her approach to teaching and learning is traditional. After all, even with the flipped classroom looming on the horizon, the traditional approach to teaching is how she learned, and it is what she knows. It is what she feels comfortable with.

She has always been in the classroom. She really has never done any remote teaching. Even her experience with tutoring was an in-person experience. Not being in the classroom is all very new. Her school cannot mandate remote learning for equity reasons. It is a small geographical area, with people packed into 1.8 square miles. The district is low income, immigrant, and largely Hispanic. They have been hit extremely hard by COVID-19. The school district services over 1,800 students in just the high school. Most of the families, about 80%, are considered essential workers. They clean hospital rooms and work at the grocery store. A lot of her students work, too. They need to work because they need to help pay the rent. It's a neighborhood that reflects social and structural inequality.

As a teacher, all she can do is try to get students to sign in online and try to get them to do some work. Her biggest challenge is crafting incentives. It is not easy. School is not mandated. Her students are teenagers and fully capable of assessing their options. In the traditional setting, she finds that the students do the work for her because they connect with her, and because the relationship they have with her, their teacher, inspires them. In the online environment, that human-to-human connection is greatly reduced. She also works as an advisor to Harvard graduate students in education. Some of the advice she gives them is that they need to find their "disco ball effect." The disco ball effect is clipped from the equation in the emergency remote learning scenario. If the content is not engaging, it is the teacher's job to get the student to complete the assignment.

Her school did have Chromebooks and they were a one-to-one school prior to the COVID-19 pandemic. They got an exceptionally large grant from the state. In the second week of the lockdown, all the kids got computers. But there were still issues: Did they have WIFI? Did the Chromebooks really work? Do they have a hotspot? They had some Chromebooks before all this occurred, but they lived in the school. They had Chromebook carts. Computers going home with these students is a quite different story.

Since school was not mandated, and it is up to each individual teacher whether he/she will be available on Zoom or not, Jennifer has chosen not to. She finds it enormously ineffective. She does post lessons on Google classroom and checks to see what is being done. This online work is not required either. The teachers do have regular meetings, a daily bulletin that comes from at least two directions, and they get info from the state. She is close to her colleagues and because the school is so large in such a small geographical district, they usually just call each other to discuss things. They just got the news last week, which was their spring break, that they were not going back this year. She is sure if they do not make the work mandatory, online engagement will plummet. Some of the students were doing something because they wanted her to know they were still trying. Overall, there is really no plan for any of this. It is up to each individual school to work out what they are going to do and how they are going to do it. The school was not ready for any of this, but they did try to get organized quickly. They have been flexible, and they did get the Chromebooks distributed.

Jennifer feels incredibly lucky to still be employed. She is a tenured teacher and feels secure in her job. She admits she is barely working. She has a school laptop. She got it last year. She admits she has no idea about compliance or any other laws governing remote work. She is not familiar with FERPA, and certainly has received no training on how this law might influence what she does working online. She describes teaching in a public school as a sticky environment anyway, so she is generally careful about what she says and to whom. In her opinion, there is not a fair way to handle this. Does she give a "pass/fail" grade to students that have been doing the work? Is it fair or not to let those students who are not passing bring up their grades? After all, they did have a lot of the term left.

She feels like she is teaching into a void and it is ridiculous. If they are not going to count quarter four, why is she putting up work on Google Classroom? If there was recognition for the work being done, both by her and her students, she would feel like there was more purpose to the job. It would give the students a reason to sign on and continue working. She does understand that the school district cannot mandate this because of equity reasons. There is no prescription for the work from home environment. The computer equipment, software, mobile phones and tablets, applications, etc. are at the discretion of the individuals, both students and teachers. The policy for teachers is "just make yourself available." No social media has always been a policy. They do not use ClassDojo, but they do use an application called Remind. It is a text-based app. Everyone has a Google account, but they do not have Gmail. They do not have school emails. She can call home or email home and try to talk to someone. Trying to communicate with students is difficult and there is no direct approach. There is no email that allows her to get in touch with all her period one students at once. To reach out, she has a combination of students' personal emails and parent emails. That is it.

Jennifer had a student sign on and complete lesson one yesterday, even though her class is officially on lesson twenty. He has been missing in action since the beginning of the year. There is no accountability for showing up or not showing up.

The expectations are loose, to say the least. There is also no way of being sure who is doing the work. She signs on sporadically and goes through the lessons and responses that collect on Google Classroom. If she does not sign on, she does not catch the work that is being done. She works with so many variables every day in the classroom. Her boss trusts her and respects her and thinks she is a good teacher, but in effect she is not working because there are just too many unknowns. The expectations and requirements are unclear. She feels like if she made phone calls, there would be no one home.

The requirements for teacher observations for performance evaluations are all based on a face-to-face classroom. Teacher evaluations have been put on hold. This does not give anyone much incentive to sign on and make themselves available if no one cares and it does not really count. She feels like a lot of teachers are being asked to "entertain" a lot of kids online all day. She is not doing that. If the work is not required and does not count, it just does not make sense to do it.

On a scale of 1 to 4, 1 being I do not want to do this anymore and 4 I love it, she would be a 1. Jennifer finds it difficult to even answer this question. She says she is not working from home; she is floating. She does not like it because she feels like she is not working. She has a ton of free time but that is because she is not really working. She has time to connect with her family and friends, more than she needs or wants. She sees many of these people working many more hours than they used to. She feels like she is out of sync with people, unproductive, instead of a productive person who contributes to society. Jennifer likes a highly structured environment where she can perform comfortably within those boundaries. She misses the structure. She describes herself as high energy. The expansiveness of the working from home environment and the general absence of structure is uncomfortable. The #WFH environment does not help her to be more productive.

Currently, she says she is just treading water. She needs more clarity, more accountability and more incentives. In Jennifer's own words, "The one thing that really matters is if kids decide to sign on that day or not. Unless you have that carrot, it does not matter if you have the most engaging lesson. If all your students wake up and decide not to show up, they won't even see it." Moving forward, if she had to continue working remotely, she thinks that having a plan, rules and structure would help. Having a clear schedule and expectations would help, too. In her opinion, the only way online education is going to work moving forward is with a plan. When does she need to contact students? What are the expectations for creating new content, assessing, and evaluating students?

When I asked Jennifer six months later, this is what she said: The start of the school year [September 2020] has been all consuming. It has been a crazy time. In the spring we were doing crisis teaching, not really real, no requirements or expectations. We wanted to be responsive and respectful that the town I teach in was hit really hard by the COVID pandemic and is still in the red zone. We are now teaching for real. Attendance is required. This pandemic has totally shifted the way we teach. All of a sudden, we are all online using new technologies, resources and engagement tools. It's all new. It's not just more Zoom calls. For teachers the actual work has changed. We have a new alternating schedule because we don't want students to be Zooming with all of their teachers all day every day. The students have more asynchronous and independent work. It's working for some students but not working for others. Teachers are working longer and harder than before because online learning takes more time and effort. Students are becoming more independent because they have to be. Teachers are changing the way they grade and how they teach because they need to, and this will shift the way we teach moving forward.

She misses the human interaction. It's difficult to create community because students are effectively inviting others into their homes. They don't know each other and establishing those connections can be difficult. It's difficult to have those personal conversations on Zoom. It's tough. Zoom all day is a lot. People get tired. Zoomed out. All schools in Massachusetts did give their teachers ten days of professional development. A lot of schools made teachers go into the classrooms and teach on Zoom from the school building. She was lucky. Although that is what her superintendent originally planned, there was so much pushback, [the superintendent] changed it. They didn't have to teach in empty classrooms that were both depressing and unsafe. Her school supported the teachers.

She misses spontaneity of being social. She misses her students. She has never seen many of them and wouldn't know them if she passed them on the street. She is trying to get everyone on camera, but it hasn't happened yet. Jennifer has no idea what her job will look like moving forward. It keeps changing. It seems like the administration, particularly the superintendent, is more interested in appearance than reality. The district might call everyone back for "optics" regardless of risk. There is a lack of trust.

Jennifer admits that she has learned a great deal as a result of being forced to go online: new tools, new tricks, new strategies and pedagogies. Her students are all digital natives and this experience has pushed teachers to engage students in new ways, to use the technology. There are no more paper handouts. She is convinced there is no going back. She would be a 2.5 now. She likes not commuting, not packing lunches or prepping meals, she likes the ease of being at home. She doesn't like having a desk job. Her body is not used to sitting in front of a screen all day and she is more irritable.

I interviewed Dave in early April 2020. He **Dave**
teaches high school, and pointed out that our
schools are babysitters. The school he teaches at is
blue collar, semi-urban and serves a wide range of
diverse students. He thinks that once the schools
start to see how much money they are saving by
going virtual, the future will look quite different.
There is a lot of funding that goes into running
buses, paying school bus drivers, manning the
cafeteria, paying lunch clerks and other activities.
He is not sure that parents will want to send their
children back into this normal school environment.
He is also not sure what the "new normal" will look
like. He is sure it is not going to look like it did before
COVID-19. Dave feels comfortable working from
home, but he misses the classroom because of the
interaction.

Dave is a department leader. He finds it hard
to believe that the technical skills of his staff are as
poor as they are. Simple things like posting links in
documents, a basic understanding of files and file
types, and saving and retrieving documents are
not part of their repertoire. They are all high school
teachers, professionals, and now they are going
remote. They are also all terribly busy. Preparing
for five classes a day is not unusual. They also have
not received much training on using technologies,
certainly not from the school district.

Dave has been doing things online for over a
decade, but he is the exception. He has also been
doing it on his own. He has his own open source
LMS. It runs on his server. He maintains it and does
the updates. The same LMS running on the school
server has not been updated in years. They are also
using Google Classroom. They use it because of

convenience. That is what the school now openly supports. If it were not for Google Classroom, going virtual would have been a total disaster even though everyone had their Chromebooks and it was a one-to-one school before the pandemic.

The other teachers in his department are doing online and trying hard to be creative and adjust but it has not been easy for them. They have maintained their creativity; it is when it comes to implementing online learning that the challenge begins. The idea of making a template on Google, sharing it and then having students fill it out and submit their own was a totally foreign concept. This kind of step-by-step preparation to use technologies is the experience that is missing. The COVID experience will change this. These kinds of things will become commonplace.

Part of the challenge is the arsenal of technologies available. There are three choices for an LMS in just one high school, maybe more. K-12 generally lacks standards in this area. It is up to the individual faculty. Students can have many different technologies to learn: websites, exam generators, adaptive learning apps, LMS, text messaging apps, the Google Suite, and on and on. Dave has spent time researching and learning different options. Since there is no official policy, he can use whatever he wants if he feels it is appropriate and safe. Most faculty have not done this kind of research; they do not have the interest or the desire. The school has a person who is their official technology coach, but he has been busy. He sends out a lot of links but not much training. Dave took it upon himself to set up a Google Classroom to organize and disseminate information. He thought this was better than hundreds of emails. It took a year to implement. Fortunately, because of his proactive nature with technologies, it was already in place when the pandemic hit.

The kids tell him that the teachers are giving them way too much work. Part of this is because in addition to the course content, they are being asked to learn all these different interfaces. David has experienced this himself with an online doctorate he is working on with a small college in California that does not have a strong instructional design group. From class to class everything is different: the syllabi, the grading, the requirements, the due dates, the interactions, the interfaces. The expectations are not clear or consistent. Students spend a lot of time and energy just trying to figure out what they need to do. The same is true in the K-12 environment.

The biggest challenge he faces is communication with his learners. There is no consistency in the tools. He is supposed to meet with seven different groups weekly. Just setting up and coordinating the links and times with everyone involved is not easy. He set up SMS text lists, emails, and calendars. At least he has the understanding to set up consistent meeting rooms for each group and not generate new links weekly; many teachers do not. Here too they use Google Meet, Zoom and whatever else someone chooses for synchronous meetings. Or was that Hangouts, Facetime, Slack, Teams or Skype? Because digital never forgets, it is more than possible to have the old codes/links and the new codes/links both out there somewhere. From the beginning he went out of his way to try to be consistent but that is because he is aware; most teachers are not.

Dave understands the importance of "chunking" content into units or weeks and set his online classes up accordingly on Google Classroom. Teachers that do not have training in online learning do not necessarily know about "chunking." Dave is trying to be flexible. Some students have not even learned how to log in yet. The school is probably going pass-fail for the spring semester, but they have not communicated this to the students. The high school set up a schedule for office hours on Monday from 11 AM to 12 noon and then each day after that two classes meet, one from 10 AM to 11 AM and the next from 11 AM to 12 noon. This accounts for the eight periods they have in the face-to-face classroom. They are focused on time, not learning.

For two weeks, the district was in limbo. They had what they called ELOs (extended learning objectives), or no new material, just content review. What they communicated to the students was that whatever work they did, it did not count and would not be graded. Guess what happened?

His school was not ready for the virtual workplace. They tried. They did the best they could. Fortunately, people have a sense of humor. They tried to follow the directives of the state. They just did not have the knowledge or experience so they held back as much as they could. Several neighboring districts went full speed ahead and then had to pull back. Dave hit some compliance issues with special needs students. He has a student that must have everything that is in written form read to her. This means he needs to create an audio file online. Accessibility online is often ignored, which is simply a lawsuit waiting to happen. Is this his responsibility or the instructional team's? He has also experienced the phenomena of Zoom bombing, porn, vaping and all. He chooses to use Google Meet with his classes because he can limit access to only the people in his classes.

State law dictates that teachers will receive an evaluation, which has been translated into "attend this meeting online." Performance evaluations and the compliance laws governing them were written for face-to-face teaching and learning. Other than teacher performance monitoring, Dave is unaware of and has never received training on any compliance issues.

He finds that teaching his Music Theory class is much better online. He has a captive audience. They have headphones on and they listen. When he teaches in a face-to-face classroom, students are distracted and all over the place. He emphasizes that this is content dependent. For some classes he feels like he can accomplish more, like Music Theory, and for some classes it is nearly impossible, like piano.

They had the equipment, sort of. They had Chromebooks. That worked for a one-to-one school when they were in the face-to-face world. They really were not as robust as what the students needed when everyone went home. Many learners use their own home computers if they have them. Then there is the issue of security. If Dave posts a YouTube video of Elvis, it is blocked for students on school computers. They try to protect students from everything. YouTube videos need to be downloaded, put on his private server and then shared. There were many restrictions that were old school and needed to be changed. Google Meet was restricted in the beginning.

Dave appreciates the freedom he has been given to do what he wants teaching online. This is not true for everyone. Not having specific directives was hard for some of his colleagues. He points out that all classes are different. The learning audiences are different and so is the content, so they require different approaches. Calculus is not gym class. He feels that the administration gave him the freedom to do what he wanted to, with just enough directive to say give us grades and monitor participation. He has about ten students who have gone missing. He hasn't heard from them even though he reaches out and sends an email every week. Online takes a lot more time. Dave wonders why there is this erroneous perception that online is easier, that it will save you time, when he has discovered that just the opposite is true. Good online learning is a lot more work. It takes a lot more thought and planning and certainly requires a lot of effort. He equates it to teaching in the dark or having a continuous substitute plan. You are not going to be where the learning is happening, but you need to make it all happen.

On a scale of 1 to 4, 1 being I do not want to do this anymore and 4 I love it, he would be a 3. He likes teaching from home, but he misses the interaction in the classroom. In a perfect world, he would want to go into the classroom a few days a week and be remote the rest of the time. Dave is convinced that the future will look something like that, he is just not sure what it will look like exactly. He appreciates saving money and a better work environment that comes from working at home. He gets to take walks with his sister and spend more time with his niece and nephew. He does not think he is working more; he does feel that it can feel that way online, especially if you are brand new to online learning. Once you develop the structure and the patterns it really is not harder or more work. He is better able to pace himself online.

What is difficult is constant change. Not knowing what is expected and having the situation in constant upheaval can be exhausting. The communications can be too much. He really has not established the boundaries he needs. He does encourage his students to make a weekly plan to do the work and stick to it. He points out that he is not going to be available late Saturday evening and encourages them to get the work done early and not wait until the last minute. He does feel that communication planning is something he will do in the future. It is a chaotic environment. He uses Remind. He does not give out his personal phone number or email. With Remind he has a record. The other side of freedom is there can be consequences to the learner and the teacher. A lot of teachers are stepping up and trying to meet the demands of teaching online, but not everybody is.

When I asked Dave six months later, this is what he said: There won't be any more snow days. We will just switch over to online and keep going. Recently our school had to close for five days because of a positive COVID case. Supposedly, we are online temporarily but who knows. I am fairly sure we will not lose days and be going until the end of June like we used to. Generally, everyone is much more aware and tuned into technology. The school has given us the software and hardware we need to do remote learning and ongoing support is being addressed. Most of my colleagues and students enjoy online and hybrid learning. Of course, there are a lot of variables and it depends on the subject being taught. I would not be surprised if, moving forward, and I have been saying this for years, when public schools learn how much money they can save on transportation, we will be online at least one day a week. The fact that schools act as babysitters has been part of the problem. The school district I am in has been very proactive in trying to support teachers all the way through this COVID crisis.

What I miss the most is the routine I had with face-to-face teaching. I miss the comfort of having things already prepared. It seems that every day there is something new that doesn't work and it is a challenge to figure out. It's difficult to say what my job will look like moving forward. There are so many variables (vaccines, politics, virus outbreaks, etc.); they all play a roll. The unknown is still driving the narrative at this point. [It is] hard to say when or if a sense of normalcy will return. Certainly, there will be a heavier use of technologies and more distance learning on some level moving forward. He is curious to see where the public school system takes this. On a scale of 1 to 4, he would be a 4 even though he is not doing remote learning from home now, he is doing a hybrid learning model. Dave loves the hybrid model. It gives him more one-on-one time with students. Those who work ahead still work ahead, and he sees high quality work. Students who don't do their work are still not doing their work, only they are not in the classroom and he doesn't have to babysit them. He said he was being brutally honest here.

I interviewed Julie in early April 2020. She is an art teacher. She teaches a combination of middle school and high school. Her district told her to give the students assignments for fun with no grading. She also adjuncts at a local college. All three institutions were not ready for the remote learning environment. No one thought they would be out as long as they were. A few weeks at the most. She still has projects to grade and return and portfolios to create. She has one student who has a seeing eye dog. She has not heard from this student because the assignments posted on the LMS are not accessible to her. The school has not made accommodations for this yet. Ultimately, it comes down to money. They have tried to make some accommodations, but they are limited. The first part of the semester when they met in person this student did all the work expected of her.

Julie has a similar dilemma with her high school students. Many of her students do not have any materials at home. About 33% of her students have not done anything. She has not heard from them. A lot of her students come from lower income families. They rent and might be facing eviction soon if they can't pay the rent. There is a divide between the "haves" and the "have nots." Many of the "have not" students also work, or they are babysitting their younger siblings.

Julie feels totally comfortable working from home. She and her partner have a sixteen-month-old, and she loves being home with the baby. She gets to spend more time with her family. She has a home office, a private space where she can work. When she is in that space, she is working. When she is not, she is not working. Julie understands the need for structure, boundaries, and a routine. She works in the morning, takes a walk and eats lunch, returns to work, and does the same routine every day. She's comfortable with it but it's not the way she likes to teach. She has virtual hours on Google Meet but very few students show up. Most students who do show up just want to connect. They show her their dog. They miss her. She misses the visual cues you get in a three-dimensional environment that you do not have online. Fortunately, she had enough time to make those connections and establish a rapport with her students before she had to go remote.

Julie sees mental health as a big challenge in the remote environment: more anxiety, more substance abuse, more issues for students and their parents. Her own emails have increased from two to fifty in a day. She posts assignments on Google Classroom and uses Canvas (a LMS) for the college. What is anxiety producing is that everything keeps changing. Every day, sometimes almost hourly, meetings get scheduled and then cancelled and then rescheduled. She is expected to be available during the regular hours of the school day, every day. She has Remind for text messaging, but did not set it up. She says she cannot really do the same level of assignments; she needs to water them down. The students get the basics, but the class is not the same quality as it was face-to-face.

Nobody thought a pandemic was going to happen, or when it did, they did not think it would last this long. Julie is in the New York/New Jersey area, which is highly populated. They thought it would be a short closure. Her district was not prepared, but everyone is doing their best.

Her district provides no hardware, software, or reimbursement for her working from home. She created her home office and paid for everything herself. New Jersey, New York and Pennsylvania currently have no laws governing the remote work environment. Human Resources is not involved, and neither is the teachers' union. Some of her teacher friends had to sign out Chromebooks from the school; some did not have WIFI. Many teachers do not have the equipment or training or confidence for teaching remotely. One teacher said he was expected to use three new platforms overnight after thirty years of face-to-face teaching. Julie says age is not the determining factor. She got her ninety-four-year-old grandmother on a synchronous discussion tool. In her mind, the key to integrating technologies is willingness and patience. Even in chaos you need patience. A lot of people are losing their patience. Time is surreal. People feel like they are in a science fiction movie.

She talks to parents more now than she ever has in the past. A friend of hers that is a special education teacher and speech specialist is really stressed. Julie doesn't have a lot of compliance issues to deal with, or at least none that she is aware of. Regardless, there was no compliance training.

A lot of students access her using their phones. That is their only access, the only internet connection they have. Julie guesses about 65% of her students use their phones for everything. Many of these kids do not have the hardware and software they need at home. Julie says that even she struggles with old equipment at home. School is where the work gets done and is really like a second home to teachers and students. Teachers also do not have what they need at home. Her principal struggles too. He was looking a little wired and tired. He is supervising a middle school where under normal conditions the classes are too big and the population is diverse and can have a wide range of issues. Many of her male colleagues look like mountain men in the remote workplace. Everyone is adapting differently. Many are not adapting at all. People are weary and tired, but everyone is doing their best. They had a hundred people on Google for a faculty meeting, with chirping birds, screaming kids, and barking dogs in the background. Department meetings are better online because there are five people. They are more manageable and less chaotic. Many things are simply different. Teacher evaluations have been put on hold. She is on her own internet. She has instructions to record all Google meetings and have another faculty member in the room with her. On a positive note, everyone had Gmail accounts and Google is the platform that most of the school is using. There are no hard rules, but at least they encourage faculty to make choices and use one family of technology for consistency.

On a scale of 1 to 4, 1 being I do not want to do this anymore and 4 I love it, Julie would be a 2.5. If she did not have a young child at home, her score would be lower. She likes elements of working from home but would like it to supplement her regular teaching. The reason she became a teacher is to make that connection with students. Julie does not feel like she is doing that in the remote workplace, at least not yet. Moving forward, Julie see changes. Maybe the schools will go to shifts, like Philadelphia did when her mother was a child. Maybe they will find a way to reduce class size, using online learning. Whatever evolves will be a balance of finances and needs.

There is a real inability to imagine something new. The leaders are hanging on to what was, and trying to handle the present, not plan for the future. People do not like to change; they gravitate toward what they know. They hang on to what is familiar and what is comfortable. With COVID-19 their worlds have changed dramatically and overnight. Julie does think that in the future teachers will use more technology because they will be more comfortable with using it. She really feels like the integration of technologies into the classroom depends on the subject and the teacher's perspective. Teachers are relatively autonomous entities and, ultimately, what happens in the classroom online or face-to-face is up to them. Neither environment is a perfect fit for everyone. Julie makes a good point that people who love technology and want to teach that way are a different population than the people who signed on to teach face to face.

When I asked Julie six months later, this is what she said: I cannot predict what will happen to education. Everything from the death of snow days (we can now teach virtually!) to perhaps a death of the SATs and standardized testing in general (which I think is long overdue anyway as it is inequitable). I'm teaching in a hybrid setting right now. The students rotate into two different cohorts (blue and gold) in person and then everyone else is virtual. My classes of 30 are split to being about 8 in person on a given day and 22 online all learning at the same time through "synchronous" learning. We don't have enough devices yet for the 1:1 and I have been getting to-go art packs together, but we just do not have enough resources. Teaching drawing and painting from a distance is hard when students only have lined paper and pens at home (if that), Right now, I'm focusing on supply distribution and flexibility. Every lesson has to be more customized.

Loss of contact with my colleagues and students is heartbreaking. In the past I would take tracing paper, grab a student's pencil and show them how to fix/enhance their art. Now the students are virtual or in person and they can't be near each other without a partition board and mask. there are no or limited sports and clubs, no homecoming, none of the excitement of the first day of school moments. It's very surreal and dystopic. I miss student interaction, live art shows, bustling classrooms and hectic hallways! It's eerie!

For my college class, Gender and Pop Culture, that's a lot more work but it's going well. I have split the class of 30 into two cohorts and am condensing my lecture and repeating it twice. The asynchronous work is much better—more meaningful. I am very intentional with the assignments. However, it's a pop culture (which means current events) class, which is challenging. With the election coming up and the recent death of RBG I can't even predict what I will be teaching and analyzing because it hasn't happened yet. Therefore, I can't prepare too much ahead of time.

All the schools I work with have tried to support us through this pandemic. They have supported as much as they can but there is so much unknown and not enough resources (physical resources and emotional support). It really is a case-by-case situation and reflective of how administration and people handle stress. Some people are better with stress than others, while some project their stress.

It has been challenging but I can't imagine the administrative pressures at this time. We are all spread very thin.

I think we will be in this hybrid model for the year (unless there's a positive case—which is likely). I think it will be a scrappy year of hybrid and some all virtual (perhaps around the flu season) until a vaccine is discovered. Also, the election will add an element to all of this. I would still be a 2.5 (I'm only above average because I had 6 months of bonus time with my toddler at home). I am able to teach and be home and spend more time with him. If he were older and in school, it would be completely different. Also, my wife is home. My friends with kids at home working are beyond stressed out. I'd like a true hybrid. I embrace [mixing] technology with in-person teaching but not like this!!

Donna   When I interviewed Donna in early April 2020, elementary school posed an even bigger challenge for her. Going online overnight has been very disruptive, not only for teachers but for staff as well. Donna is a K-5 Curriculum Director. She plans curriculum, meets with students and teachers, and does workshops and in-services and trainings. It has been a very strange experience. Most of the events she planned for spring 2020 have been cancelled. She had a literacy night scheduled face-to-face for parents and teachers and now that is cancelled. Some events she has tried to take online, but with marginal success. She is still trying to stay connected with teachers, students and families and plan for next year. She does a lot of paperwork and that part of her job she can do from anywhere. She does teacher observations in the classroom, but she can no longer do that. Performance reviews and setting goals with staff members for next year has also been cancelled. She also made regular visits to classrooms, which she is not doing remotely.

The biggest challenge she is facing is trying to meet the diverse needs of the students. Each family situation is different. Donna wants to provide enough materials so that everyone has something to do but not so much that families that do not have the technologies or connections and resources are overwhelmed. She is a highly organized and structured administrator and keeps a tight schedule and calendar. The online environment is more open and freer. At school she would have had 25 things done by lunch; at home she feels like it's maybe not as many. Phone calls, text messages and emails go on all day long.

Every teacher has a school laptop, but they do not have webcams. They polled the teachers a few years ago and they voted, because of privacy concerns, not to get cameras on the computers. Now they wish they had. Teachers are running their synchronous classrooms on phones or their personal home computers. Of course, it gets even more complicated if those teachers have their own children at home. The situation can get very sticky. Plans are to change out those computers and get everyone new ones. They also put effort into using materials and supplies the students may have at home. Equity is a big issue.

Donna uses her personal phone for all her work communications. She uses Google for everything for school. They also use Zoom and Webex but not as much as Google Classroom, Meet, Drive, you name it. Typical of a school district that did not have a plan, they are using three different synchronous platforms, several different text messaging platforms including ClassDojo and Remind, and a host of other technologies including Twitter and Facebook. There is not really a centralized approach. They have created a page on their website for official links.

The district did try to rein in the number of resources being used by teachers because, even though they had good intentions, it became overwhelming for the students and their families. People are on overload. K-5 is one of the most difficult work from home environments. It takes the devotion of a parent who is capable, competent, and committed to make it work. Not every child is that lucky. The teacher's knowledge and comfort level with technology also varies widely. Some teachers are not doing anything new with content or assessment. They are concerned about the social and emotional connections with the children and their families. At least K-5 students usually have one teacher. In middle school through higher ed., a student can have six or more teachers and everyone is doing something different if there is no plan. They all may be using Google Classroom or Canvas or Blackboard but every class has a different layout, interface, and requirements. The teachers have a range of comfort levels, abilities and interests in remote learning and technologies.

Again, in this environment, and because of equity issues, internet connectivity is a concern. Many students did not have home computers. They did use computers in the school and were a one-to-one, but students did not usually take the computers home. After a few weeks of COVID-19 lockdown, the school offered students their in-school computers to check out. But just because they had the devices did not mean they had internet access. They are trying to develop a plan for allowing people to borrow internet hotspots, but that all takes time. They do not have time.

Special Education is the biggest challenge for Donna when it comes to compliance issues. They are trying to hold individual meetings virtually and figure out where these students will be placed next year. Our public school systems provide much more than education, they offer a lot of different support structures to students and families. Having these support structures available and functioning in a remote workplace has been a real challenge. The Child Online Parent Protection Act (COPPA) is something that Donna is aware of, but it is not familiar with. Services like ESL, counseling, language development and all the other supports offered by the school during the normal course of operations have had to find a way to go online almost overnight with no plan, no training and limited guidance.

Donna has what she needs to work from home from a hardware and software standpoint. Most of it is her own equipment and at her own expense. She does a lot of communication on the phone via text messaging and the phone is her own private device. So far, security has not been a problem.

On a scale of 1 to 4, 1 being I do not want to do this anymore and 4 being I love it, she would be a 3.0. She likes working from home. For the paperwork part of her job, she said remote works simply fine. The other part is interaction with people, and she does not feel that part is sustainable. She feels like she has more time working from home. She has no interruptions. She has enough room at home that she can have a private office and her daughter and husband have their own private spaces too. Her daughter, who is in the eighth grade, goes to a private school that had a plan and already had a lot of online policies, procedures, and resources in place. The teachers already had all their lessons online and the students already had portal access and laptop computers. The transition was almost seamless. They purposely do not schedule anything between 11 AM and 1 PM so that people can get offline and go outside. They take walks together every day. Donna feels like everything has slowed down and she has more time for her family, and they have more time for each other.

When I asked Donna six months later, this is what she said: I did not talk to Donna six months later. She never responded to my emails or calls. I suspect she was still terribly busy and overwhelmed.

Mark teaches third grade. If that were not **Mark**
challenging enough, he teaches children with
special needs. When I interviewed Mark in early April
2020, he said, "There is a gap between the abilities
of different students in my classroom and that is
even more interesting with distance learning." He
is a pioneer in using technology for connections
in the K-12 classroom. He is the first to admit that
there is a different connection that happens in the
face-to-face classroom and a lot of nuance is lost
in relationships connecting virtually. In his words,
there is an up and a downside to everything. He is
comfortable working from home but is concerned
about the relationships he has built with his students
and how their performance will be affected. The
longer his students are required to connect only
virtually, the price of that loss in relationships goes
higher. It all depends on the individual.

Mark has done a lot of learning online. He
is used to the online environment. He got his
undergraduate and graduate degrees online. He
prefers the synchronous environment because
there are more cues, more spontaneity. It is also
happening live. He likes people being together. He
does value the asynchronous environment because
it eliminates space and time. It allows you to work
when you want to work. You are not bound by time
or place. There is less clock anxiety. You can think
about your responses and reflect upon them.

His audience is special, but fortunately they
have Mark. He has twenty-one students all with
separate IEPs (Individualized Education Plans).
Many of his students have behavior issues and he is
afraid they will regress because they are back in the
environment that often helped to create the issues

to begin with. The gains he made with the students to help them to function independently in a group and social environment are disappearing. Every parent has become a co-teacher, and everyone is different and has a different relationship with their children. Mark surveyed his parents to see if what he was doing was working. He reports some of his parents were experiencing extreme fatigue. Now they have a full-time job; their children are being home schooled. They are full time teachers now. Many have full time jobs in addition. Many have several children.

Mark finds that they do not need to be online as much. He discovered that a lot of this is perception. Some children raise their hand often, some never do. He also found that he calls on the same children. It is a classroom of one from the parent's perspective. To get the assignments out Mark shared a Google document which lists all the assignments. He continues to add new entries by moving the new to the top and pushing the last week to the bottom. It is the same document every week and parents can go back and see the prior assignments, and use same link every week, which provides the same access and less confusion. He puts it on ClassDojo, Google Classroom and emails it. He simplified his approach for the parents.

Many of these parents use their phones for access. He is a big fan of ClassDojo. He appreciates the privacy aspect of the app and that it is COPPA (Children's Online Privacy Protection Act) compliant. It is a safe space to provide student work and pictures and it has a messaging feature. He does a video chat every morning at 9 AM and goes over the lessons for the day. He connects again at 2 PM to see if there are any issues or problems that need to be resolved. He also puts the students into breakout rooms and has them talk with each other and trusts that they do not need to have an adult in there with them. He believes they need to be in small groups and talk to each other.

Mark is a veteran at this and so are his students. They have had interactions with students in Argentina, India, Bangladesh, Ireland, and South Africa. He teaches respect. The children have learned that when other kids dress funny, speak funny or laugh funny, they still need to be mindful of what they say and do to others. This environment is not new to these children. They come to the remote learning environment with a full set of digital rules and behavioral expectations. Mark is also aware of the rules about posting links, sharing, compliance and security. He does not let the children change their names online, even though he admits it might be fun. He also has rules about leaving the room and coming back in, which he and the students adhere to.

One of his biggest challenges is coaching a child or a parent to use the technologies, hardware and software through a different lens; some are on mobile devices, some iPads, some PCs, some android, some Windows, some iOS, some old and new. He schedules a one-on-one with each student to just talk at the end of the morning and afternoon meetings. He also talks to the parents, where he coaches and supports them.

Mark designed the structure and activities his class engages in. The other two third grades look vastly different. This is one of the challenges in K-12 education: Teachers are used to doing whatever they want to do, so if you had three children in grades K-5 you would have three vastly different approaches to online learning. In Mark's own words, "It is a mindset issue." He enjoys the power of being able to do what he wants in his classroom, online or off. So do the other teachers.

Mark's district has gone with a positive approach for grading during the COVID-19 pandemic. Grades can only go up; they cannot go down. They admit they do not really know what is going on at home or in the online environment. Teachers will no longer be evaluated, there will be no state tests, and there is no accountability. The final marking period in spring 2020 is pass-fail.

Independence has two sides. There are five hundred and forty-nine independent school districts in the state of New Jersey, which is where Mark lives. There are five hundred in Pennsylvania, which is where I live. That is over a thousand different districts between the two states. Nearly everyone has a full-time superintendent, a locally elected school board, buildings, and heating bills. They range in size from a few hundred students to more than a hundred thousand. Some are good and some are not as strong. Each one is making their own decisions on what 3rd grade looks like and how students are graded. Not all states are like this. Maryland for example has twenty-three counties and the city of Baltimore school district.

It is difficult to make changes in the K-12 school system. Closing and merging schools is unpopular.

There are deep divides in the districts academically, racially, and financially. The taxes and teachers' salaries can vary widely across districts even if they are located next to each other. State officials are not encouraging mergers, and neither are the teachers' unions. However, online education could change everything.

The control balance has shifted to where the kids can ignore Mark if they want to. He is making sure that does not happen. He is bringing in guest speakers from all over the world and getting the parents involved in presenting too. They have connected with pen pals in Memphis, TN three times. All of this is because Mark understands online and understands his learners and the effort is takes to engage in a detached environment. He has them read aloud and is on the third book in a series of five.

On a scale of 1 to 4, 1 being I do not want to do this anymore and 4 I love it, he would be a 3. He does not really want to return to the classroom at the time of this interview because he is worried that teachers might try to shove 10 weeks of learning into the remaining school term. He is genuinely concerned about the social and emotional states of the children. He misses the social interaction, but he is not suffering by teaching online. He does not miss the half-hour commute or the faculty meetings or grade level meetings. There is so much time wasted in the traditional classroom. He can give more one-to-one feedback online and get more done working from home.

He has children at home who are college age. WIFI is the big challenge at home. There is no using the microwave because it interrupts the connection. Moving forward, Mark sees changes in how learning is paced and delivered. Some of his students have done better online, they have done more work, taken assignments further and feel more independent. They are showing self-motivation and they are happier, healthier, and less distracted. He thinks these are attributes schools need to keep. He thinks we need to look at blended learning. Snow days are a thing of the past.

When I asked Mark six months later, this is what he said: There are some big shifts in the direction that education will take now and in the future. We may be rushing back into hybrid openings, or all virtual, but technology has taken on a new role in the delivery of education instead of enhancing it. Student agency and autonomy have become big levers where struggle and learning differences used to control and dominate the differentiation conversations. I have had a lot of support from my administration but that does not prevent a deep sense of isolation and disconnection. The problem is that there are too many problems and not enough people who are solely focused on solving them. I am such a singular outlier I often slip between the cracks.

What I miss most about the physical classroom environment is I created a warm and inviting physical space for my students to escape to. They would enter, a fireplace was playing on the big screen, classical music was playing softly, and I never turned on the overhead lights but instead used lamps and those lights on strings like at fairs and used car lots. We collectively designed our class and set up the furniture to create a living room center with a loveseat and bean bag chairs. I miss having that kind of control over setting the stage for learning and anxiety control. I log on every morning with 22 kids at 8:45 and we work together until 10:30. It is too long developmentally, [even though] I have breaks built in, but parents have misconceptions about online learning. I spend the rest of the day developing content, posting to learning platforms, fielding parent and student communications about technology difficulties or academic struggles, etc.

The pandemic is going to have a long lasting impact on educational policies for years to come. Learning options will develop and innovation will have a hand in changing what teaching and learning looks like. Technology and pedagogy will go through major revisions. Equity has become a real topic and the need for schools to help the economy function should change how the teaching profession is run and paid for. Sadly, a major amount of highly skilled educators and administrators will leave due to the detrimental long-term impacts of all this change and stress. With them will go a wealth of knowledge that cannot be replaced. In their vacuum many mistakes will occur. The issue of educational funding will become an even more politicized issue than it already is. Public tax dollars are too tempting for the inevitable money grab not to occur. If I had to pick a number, I would still be a 3.

Jack is a firefighter and engineer in the San Francisco Bay area. He works in forty-eight-hour shifts and responds to 911 calls for a variety of issues including redwood fires, car accidents and other situations where people find themselves in trouble. He a first responder. When I interviewed Jack in early April 2020, he said, "I have two homes, the fire company and my home-home." Both situations have changed because of the COVID-19 pandemic. At the fire company, Jack had never used video chats, messaging or conference calls, now he does and does it regularly. They do daily group chats, afternoon chats and training sessions, as well as planning. He has union meetings from home, which is brand new. His biggest challenge is the time.

Work is so different now. There is a lot more anxiety. One of his daughters had anxiety issues anyway. Now he is a full-time firefighter and a substitute teacher for his girls. His wife is home, but she is a teacher, so she is online with her students too. They had to buy a few new computers because they needed four but they only had one. They did not have a lot of technology at home. Just getting everything up and running was stressful. He misses the face-to-face contact and especially the onsite trainings. He takes pride in taking training classes and then coming back and sharing what he learned with his fire department or the county. He feels like he is missing out.

His interactions are dramatically different. He goes to work at 7 AM on day one and checks in at 8:15 AM. He used to have time for physical fitness but now there is a department mandate that, three times a day, they disinfect the fire engine and the common areas they touch, like door handles

Chapter 8

The Hamster Wheel

Jack

and light switches. Much of the repetitive and redundant efforts, like the cleaning protocol, are at ridiculous and stressful levels. The directive is to clean the engine three times a day whether it goes out or not and whether anyone has been on it or not. They are cleaning the engine just to clean it. It is a waste of time and supplies, but it keeps everyone busy. The COVID situation has created a lot of fear in a work environment that is high stress to begin with. The clothes they wear on the fire engine they do not wear into the station, which they did before. They have new outfits that are bright green and can be disinfected, and masks and shields that they need to wear on medical calls, which can be a bit overwhelming. They are required to wear masks inside the fire engine but not inside the fire station. A lot of stations did not have enough protective gear for everyone, and there were other shortages. He also struggles with questions he asks himself like, "Is this a COVID patient we are responding to?" He has had a few close calls and questionable situations.

Fire departments nationwide tend to be old school. Fire departments in general do not accept change easily. According to Jack, many were not ready for online, especially at this scale. National disasters they are ready for, but working from home, not so much. Like everyone else, they are doing the best they can. All new employee training was cancelled.

The number of emails has greatly increased on all levels. So many changes had to be implemented so quickly—new technologies, new policies, new gear—it has been overwhelming in a job that can be overwhelming anyway. It all happened so fast. They have committees, unions and subcommittees. They have a COVID committee and it has branches. There is a lot of communication and a lot of meetings. It is just too much. Promotions have not gone through. Budgets are on hold. Generally, there is a degree of discomfort at all levels. Compliance and legal issues are discussed in rumblings and rumors. There's anxiety and more anxiety.

Compliance and legal issues come from all levels, local, state and federal. How they respond to a call has changed because of COVID-19. Some of the technology is up to date. For example, they just got a new dispatching program that is all touch screen, which of course they cannot use with the pandemic. Some of the technology is old. Jack equated it to the black and green screens from the past. They still use maps and they still use a lot of paper. Like in a lot of other remote jobs, personal equipment is being used for work. When a call comes in, often the firefighters are using Google maps for the GPS location. They have official phones and iPads on the fire engines, provided by a third-party company. They have a special secure network. Every engine has its own WIFI hotspot, but the phones provided are flip phones. Jack feels like this could be a wake-up call for embracing technology and moving into the future.

On a scale of 1 to 4, 1 being I do not want to do this anymore and 4 I love it, Jack would be a 2. His job as a firefighter is unique. There is no question that it requires a face-to-face component. The change has been disruptive and happened quickly. He does not feel the training online is nearly as good as it is face-to-face. Most of all he misses the face-to-face contact and social interaction. He feels reluctant to hug his kids. It is awkward and disconnected. It is a big difference between what he is doing now and what he usually does. The activities are different and the relationships with family and friends have been impacted greatly. His son's baseball season was disrupted, and his daughter's swim team practice is on hold. Normally he does not see the kids as much as he does now because now they are home from school. So is his wife. Everybody is home all day every day. The house is small, and privacy is nonexistent.

Jack's big concern is that this plays on people's nerves, and his fellow employees are becoming a little lax. He worries about his promotion and his ability to motivate others. When you are a firefighter focus is especially important. Everyone is concerned about bringing the virus home and exposure. People are getting tired of this and it has only been two months. If they only knew the long road ahead. Trust is also an issue and lack of trust just raises the anxiety level even more. It is unnerving and tense. They do a good job at the firehouse but what about when the person goes home? They are not contact tracing, and they are not monitoring. Then there is the issue of personal rights and where work stops and private life begins. Can work force you to take your temperature when you are off?

When I asked Jack six months later, this is what he said: My career has been impacted by the lack of the personal interactions We have become aware of the benefit to us and our decisions [about] face-to-face meetings. We've had profoundly serious department issues and the meetings have been done through Zoom.

The loss of in-person contact has left our fire department with an emotionless feeling. We have incredibly significant personnel issues in the department and major budget cuts looming. These Zoom meetings haven't allowed the true emotion to come through. On the flip side I feel it's allowed some people who tend to shy away from conversation in the large group setting to have a voice. It's clear some co-workers are far more comfortable speaking through online video chat forums vs. live personal meetings. The department has continued to "overstock" and prepare us for a COVID resurgence should it occur.

With the lack of real emotion being felt and a sense of disconnect, our Fire Chief and some of his staff are now coming to individual firehouses or calling "group" meetings at a safe distance "face to face" to discuss the topics and significant frustrations of our department and workforce. We never thought with the remote meetings in place and us still adhering to strict COVID protocols we'd be having meetings like this. [It is] a big change for us and our daily operations.

I miss my sense of freedom, the feeling of being able to go places and not worry about exposure and what might happen. As things slowly open back up, my family has been very reserved in public settings. I've also noticed many friends still are very reserved and hesitant to do any social events with us, because of my job. That's been more difficult for my children. My wife, Jessica, and I understand, but it's hard to explain to a seven- and a nine-year-old why certain friends don't visit or why we can't see them right now.

The implications for my job in the short and long term are unknown. My fire department remains one of the most aggressive and strict in our county in regard to PPE (Personal Protective Equipment) and policy. We have some of the strictest public and in-firehouse PPE policies. It is really starting to wear on the workforce physically and emotionally.

I believe for my fire department, it's finally brought to their attention the need for proper decontamination. We get comfortable and lazy and oftentimes have no problems coming to work battling a common cold or flu. This has brought to light being better [about] cleaning common areas and also staying home if you are sick. Unfortunately, our city pays out annually a "Sick Leave Buyout." It's an incentive to not use sick leave and receive a "bonus like" check every January. Many would drag themselves to work multiple times a year just to get that extra check. I feel this has changed some of that mindset. Jack said he would now be a 2 or may even a 1.

Yvonne works for a large healthcare organization as an administrator. When I interviewed her in early April 2020, she said she has been with the organization for twenty years. She is not comfortable working from home. She finds it distracting. She likes the structure of the office. Her husband is disabled. He has been home since 2010 and now they are both home and together. She likes a quiet working environment where she can concentrate and now she can hear the television from rooms away. It is challenging. So are the interruptions like "Are you through yet?" or "What are we having for lunch?" She is adamant about setting a schedule every morning and sticking to it. She manages nine staff members. If the staff goes into the main office, she or the manager must be there. They rotate and take turns going in. The payroll staff must go into the office because the systems require them to be onsite. The payroll staff are hourly, and the systems are old. They are not completely automated, and they have a lot of paper going back and forth between their facilities. They still have a lot of processes that are done manually.

This is her first experience working from home. Her department is based in HR, and tracks people movement and processes payroll every two weeks for the entire organization. The organization is large with about 13,000 workers, 5,000 of which are hourly employees. They have a half a dozen hospitals and many ancillary clinics. One of the biggest challenges for her in the remote environment is that she misses the collaboration and comradery of the face-to-face working environment. Walking into the office next door, drinking coffee together and having face-to-face meetings cannot be replaced on Zoom or any

Yvonne

117

other synchronous platform. It is just not the same. She misses her team.

Her organization is not cloud based and Yvonne doesn't have the same access to information at home as she does in the office. Some of what is stored on a local shared drive she cannot access from home. They have systems that are not integrated. For example, the time management system and scheduling systems do not talk to each other. They are trying to upgrade and integrate systems. They are open 24/7 365 days a year. Prior expectations for workers were no matter what—bad weather, personal crisis—there are no excuses because healthcare is open. COVID-19 changed that because the mayor was issuing stay at home orders for the entire city. The non-patient-facing workers were now allowed to work from home.

Human resources quickly developed a work from home guide and contracts. They made the staff sign work from home agreements. These included the equipment that was in the homes of the staff and how it was used and by whom. They outlined the suitability of the position for remote work and the relationships to other team members' ability to work from home. Because they are in healthcare, they were extra aware of COVID-19 exposure and the exposure risks for essential workers who could not work from home. For the most part the organization was not prepared for the remote workplace, although in some areas, like transcription, newer younger workers had already pushed the boundaries and were working remotely. Some other areas like IT, informatics, and analytics had already moved to a split week of two days in the office and three working remotely. Yvonne sees more of this in the future now that many people have experienced the remote workplace. The company provides hotspots, printers and laptops to remote workers. Up to now the work was mostly siloed and segmented but now the remote workplace has grown.

Cyber security is a huge concern in regard to patient records, payroll and healthcare in general. IT handles security, compliance and HIPA (Healthcare Information Privacy Act) standards. They have dual authentication, bit codes and portal entry. However, they still have an incredibly old school approach to trust. Employees, or associates as they are referred to, do data entry and are not really trusted to get the job done without supervision, maybe because they are hourly and maybe because the pay is not the best. Or maybe because it is a cultural climate that values medical professionals like doctors and nurses differently than it does hourly workers. There is a lack of trust and a fear that people working from home will not get the job done. Internet security and time management are both big concerns. Nevertheless, they still SMS chat over their personal phones and have weekly meetings on Microsoft Teams using their own mobile phones. They also use their own networks and data plans. They have secure access to the company email on their cell phones using an app, MobileIron, that requires dual authentication, but other chat communication is over their own personal networks.

Yvonne likes to keep work and home separate. It affects her mood and personality. She understands that she has a home personality and a work personality. She would rather keep the two worlds apart. One of her associates had a home break-in where equipment was stolen. The perpetrators could not do anything with the laptops they stole because of the security in place but it was emotionally unsettling for the associate. She felt guilt and shame even though it was nothing she could have controlled.

On a scale of 1 to 4, 1 being I do not want to do this anymore and 4 is I love it, Yvonne would be a 2.5. She feels like her family loves it. Her husband has some serious health problems. Her daughter helps with his care, and they feel comforted by having Yvonne working from home. If it weren't for her family, she would much rather be in the office. She prefers that working environment and she likes being able to separate rather than blend the two. She appreciates the flexibility of working from home. She does not think we are going back to the workplace we once knew. In her opinion, in healthcare the new workplace is a remote workplace if you are not a patient-facing employee.

She feels like employers will create a better balance for people in the remote environment and people will get used to it, just like they got used to taking their shoes off at the airport after 9/11. Yvonne says that COVID-19 has shaken up the way we do so many things but there is a silver lining in this if we look for it. The examples she gives are regular, reoccurring doctor appointments for her husband that are now telemedicine appointments. She can do that all virtually now. It's freed up a lot of her time from going back and forth to appointments and sitting in waiting rooms, but it has also given her husband a sense of calm, with less anxiety and less stress.

When I asked Yvonne six months later, this is what she said: Yvonne never returned my emails or phone calls. COVID has been so hard on everyone, especially healthcare.

Mitch is an executive with an oil company giant. When I interviewed him in early April 2020, he explained that, after a few oil spills here and there, they have a company culture that encourages safety and training. Mitch works in the learning and development area. He is concerned with surveys on evaluation and effectiveness. He sees training budgets favoring online training going forward, and budgets for travel to and from instructor-led training decreasing. Many of the jobs in large oil companies are dangerous. In Mitch's opinion, people who work out on the terminals and in shipping need instructor-led training. In the future, the challenge will be to make that kind of training virtual. He thinks training for senior level executives will remain face-to-face. Like with everything else, COVID-19 will have an impact.

He has had the flexibility and the opportunity to work from home because much of what he does faces a computer screen. It was extremely comfortable for Mitch to move to a totally remote environment. He had experience and his job expectations were clear. The transition was easy. He does have a level of discomfort, though, working from home. Mitch is talking to me from his home office and points out the intrusive feeling he has about having colleagues come into his home. He has furniture stored in his office because he is doing some painting and remodeling at home, since he is at home anyway. He's redoing his bedroom and doesn't feel comfortable because the company now has access to his private space, some personal areas of his life. He recognizes he is sharing more of his personal "stuff" in the remote home environment than he did at the worksite. There can be barking dogs, playful children and noisy neighbors.

Mitch sees staying focused on the job as the biggest challenge working from home. He is about half and half in terms of what he prefers, working from home vs. the office. There are situations where he would prefer to be in the office and others where he does not mind being at home. Like many of his colleagues, he misses the interactions and the spontaneity of intermingling with other coworkers an office environment supports. When you are in the office and you need to go talk to Joe, you walk down the hall to Joe's office and that is it, you talk to Joe, right then and there, on the spot. At home, you must make a phone call, start a meeting or open an application. He also sees inconsistencies in the technologies and connections. In Mitch's words, it needs to be improved. He sees security, hacking and reliability as areas of opportunity for his company to grow.

Mitch schedules calls and makes appointments. In between those interactions, he is out back working in his garden or working on his remodeling projects. This is the part of working from home Mitch likes. He points out that his "Honey Do List" of projects that need his attention around the house has exploded. His workday is less structured now than when he was in office. In the office he was more sequestered or trapped or constricted. At home it is easy to go outside or go to the kitchen for snack. He finds the scheduled meetings more focused and admits the connection virtually is different. He finds people are more in a hurry to get to the point, get it done and get it over with. His finds that the meetings are shorter but there tend to be more of them. A lot of these meetings are more about connection than meaningful issues.

According to Mitch, Big Oil was ready for this change, and they support their workers working from home. They have all the equipment, network connections and technologies they need. They have company cell phones equipped with apps but mostly they use the company laptop for business meetings. The technologies they use to connect are the same technologies they used before COVID-19 sent the workforce home. Both the synchronous platform and the collaboration app were installed, and they had been using them in the office. Going remote did not require learning new technology.

Much like the production floor in manufacturing, the front-line workers at the terminals and loading docks cannot work from home. It is the office workers who can and are well supplied. These folks enter the company systems via a portal and sign-on looks exactly like it did in the office. Behind that wall, the systems, interface layout and all other aspects are the same. Behind the firewall, they could be anywhere: at their desk, at the beach or in the family room.

Compliance is a big concern at Big Oil, and ergonomics is taken seriously. In the face-to-face environment, a staff member measures the height of your desk and observes you working. This is all lost at home. Big Oil, maybe because of its history, is very aware of worker safety. They start every meeting with a safety topic and spend a few minutes just reminding people of the importance of safety. They do this on video conferences as well. Every meeting starts with a safety moment.

Mitch's boss is in Texas, and he is in California, so remote is nothing new for their relationship. Mitch is comfortable with working from home and his boss is fine with it. The company culture is supportive. The culture values individual worker contributions and has a positive attitude toward trust in the workers. Everyone is encouraged to speak up and has the authority to stop work if they see an issue of health and safety or something that is dangerous. Visibility and appreciation are a different story. The culture supports the individual worker in career choices and advancement. It is the worker's choice to work overtime and go beyond limitations. When the worker is remote it is more difficult to show those attributes. The people you need to impress and influence to move up the corporate ladder are also not as available, and you are not as visible in the remote workplace. The recently redid their performance evaluation process, and they now have quarterly evaluations, biannual and annual reviews. They no longer have numerical rankings and now managers have a pool of funds to apply to merit increases. So far, being remote has not been an issue.

On a scale of 1 to 4, 1 being I do not want to do this anymore and 4 I love it, Mitch would be a 3. He likes working remotely but feels like he needs to be in the office to engage face-to-face for some issues. He is an individual contributor and does not have a staff reporting directly to him. He does work with various departments and leaders around the company to address training and development challenges. He likes working from home. He thinks the company will do more of this in the future. They will not be going back to the way things were before COVID forced the remote workplace.

Mitch says the impact on his family life has been positive, except for the expanded "Honey Do List"! He does not have kids. He and his wife share the space and it works well. He has more free time and more flexibility which has a positive and negative side. Did he have more free time in the office? Or does he have more downtime at home? He finds the work-life boundaries are respected and the regular work hours are effective limits for most communications.

Moving forward, things will be different. He sees a lot more remote work in the future. They currently work every other Friday, and Mitch feels that soon the company will have a four-day week. He thinks they will examine each position and if you were effective working from home, you will be able to continue that in the future. This will save the company money on facility management and save the employees a commute. Mitch expects a split shift, with a few days in the office and a few days at home. He can get as much done working from home in 3 or 4 hours a day as he was working in the office for 8 hours a day. He sees staff reductions and decreases in salaries. He thinks time off and vacation policies will also be examined. More jobs will be telecommuting jobs and there will be an emphasis on knowledge over time spent or the hourly worker. This journey into the remote workplace will eventually affect the very nature of work. People will work on a project, have requirements and expectations, and be paid for completions. He feels that Big Oil is in a solid position to adapt and will adapt soon.

When I asked Mitch six months later, this is what he said: My company has supported remote work for a long time so not much has changed. In the future, I think there will be an increasing move out of densely populated downtown locations in high-rises to more campus-type accommodations and greater use of temporary office environments (like WeWork) when face-to-face meetings are necessary. I miss the office and my colleagues. There are in-person dynamics (body language, aside exchanges, etc.) that just can't be replicated in remote situations. Remote meetings have to be more scripted. What I miss most about life prior to the shutdown in March is going to the movies and free food at Costco.

I am not sure what my job looks like in 2020 or 2021. I am sweating out a big layoff, maybe making a job change. On the upside, I can consider jobs in locations that I would not have before because of the increasing move to remote work. It is accelerating a lot of things already in play: increased flex work arrangements, remote meetings (cutting travel costs), and a move to the 4-day work week. Everybody will be wearing face masks and not shaking hands. I am still a 3, mostly because I somewhat of an introvert and can tend to my garden more.

This response was received on September 22, 2020. A few weeks later, I found out from one of Mitch's friends he had been let go. Mitch joined the ranks of the unemployed because of COVID-19. Even Big Oil was hit hard.

Danielle works for a Fortune 500 insurance company in technology support. She manages a small group of people. When I interviewed Danielle in early April 2020, she said that, a few years ago, she and her team worked from home because the company was redecorating the office. Everyone did fine despite the fact they were a little anxious initially. Danielle decided then that she would be flexible about working remotely if people needed to for reasons like a sick kid, the cable guy or just general focus and mental health. This time around she felt confident. She does recognize that full time remote is different than occasionally working from home. It's one thing to do it on a Friday every few weeks and it's totally different when you do in every day, day in and day out.

Some of the biggest challenges she sees are having a dedicated workspace set up that meets your needs. She cleaned off her craft desk and created an office desk. She bought a bigger screen, mouse and keyboard, and is not just using the laptop from the company anymore. The ability to work from anywhere only works for the short term; for the longer term she discovered the need for a comfortable and dedicated work environment. The technology has had challenges too: double screens, headsets, internet connections and printers.

Interactions for Danielle have evolved. She gets together with her team members twice a week and does a one-on-one with each of them weekly. Originally, she did all the one-on-ones on the same day, Thursday, but found that to be a bit much. She now talks to someone on her team every day because she wants that kind of connection. She feels like she has a lot of meetings, maybe more now

Danielle

than before. She starts her day intentionally. She does the commute up the stairs and then begins her workday. She finds this purposeful beginning much better and her attention to work is more focused and intentional. She schedules at least an hour a day for lunch and tries to get away from the computer. She puts it on her daily schedule in a specific color. In the workplace she would go to the cafeteria and then go back to her desk and eat, check emails, etc., but at home she finds she really needs to get away from that screen regularly at lunchtime. She also finds that phone connection is different than the computer connection. She keeps her phone with her, but she intentionally takes a real lunch break.

Her company is incredibly supportive. They went out early with COVID-19. They started working from home March 16, 2020. Compliance is another issue. She has staff that have small children and the pandemic has been exceedingly difficult for them. Signatures and storage were an initial challenge. They changed a lot of the requirements for physically signing quickly. There are some restrictions on what states you can work from and where you can work because of insurance industry regulatory compliance issues. She also cannot forward mail to a personal email address. The reason for both is information privacy. Once she is in the company systems, she cannot print anything to her personal printer.

She has a company cell phone. She tries to use it exclusively for business. She encourages her workers to use the company equipment for company business. There are a few exceptions for personal mobile devices but not many, and those require a liability release. The company runs through

Cisco and everyone is on a VPN. She also thinks that it is easier to step away from your job if you can put the company phone (her iPhone) down and pick up your personal device (her Android).

She has been in her job a long time. Her boss feels amazingly comfortable with her working from home. She misses the face-to-face communication and connection. She feels like she had a better relationship and less job frustration when she could communicate with her boss in the office. The organization has a clear mission statement, and it is clearly communicated. So far, security has only been an issue for the implementation of Microsoft Teams. They rolled it out quickly, in about two weeks. To operationalize it, Danielle had to use three different devices, one for video, one for dial in and one for storage. She is sure that over time it will get better. Prior to COVID-19 they used video but not regularly. Now they have a host of different platforms and connections from Webex (which they had originally) to Teams, GoToMeeting and Zoom. Every interface is a little different and it is all rather new. Connections have been an issue and just about everyone experiences some frustration and a learning curve. She believes everyone feels more stress when technology does not work at home.

On a scale of 1 to 4, 1 being I do not want to do this anymore and 4 I love it, Danielle would be a 3. Her husband and children are at home. Everybody is home and her children are grown so she really is not impacted that much. However, she misses the face-to-face connections with people. She wants to get back to the office but feels she is saving a lot of time and money working from home. She uses less clothes, has lower dry cleaner bills and spends less on restaurants. She also feels like she gets a lot more done and is more productive. However, her personal affairs are impacted by her inability to sign off at the end of the day. She feels that constant pull to be connected and available for her team and organization. She does think she is working more working from home. She would like it to be more flexible but does not really find that to be true. She feels restricted by her workday mentality. There is a feeling of guilt about taking a walk in the middle of the day that she would not experience in the office. The area of trust comes up again. She has developed a routine where she puts the equipment away over the weekend and brings back the craft desk, so that she really does sign off and disconnect. This helps.

Danielle feels less comfortable with the new people. She tries to give everyone the benefit of the doubt but struggles a little. She tries to be open and understanding. They don't use video chat much, but phone calls have increased and so has text messaging. She created a personal account to connect with her team and used everyone's personal phone numbers, so that they have a place for simple personal interactions where they can send photos and share. She works hard to keep the human connection. Danielle understands human morale and the importance of worker mental health.

Moving forward, she sees flexibility as a byproduct of seeing the ability to be productive in the remote environment. She thinks we will re-think work. She thinks the workplace will look quite different. There will be fundamental changes in personal connection and trust. She hopes this will be reflected in the company culture and new processes that are more expedient and convenient and flexible, and that work from the remote workplace will be adopted in the office culture.

When I asked Danielle six months later, this is what she said: Danielle did not respond to my emails or phone calls. Working from home short term was one thing. Adjusting to the remote workplace longer term is something else. I am really not sure why she did not respond. I know it is easy to lose an email when you are getting an avalanche of online communications every day.

Los Angeles is probably one of the worst cities in the United States for commuters. Everybody does it and nobody likes it. When I interviewed Nathan in early April 2020, he had been in the voiceover business for decades. He lives just outside of Hollywood, and although he works from home, he still needs to be close by the studios. Marketing, advertising and acting is how he makes his living. Although he has an agent, he is primarily in business for himself and has a first-class studio in his home. He had a studio in Universal City for about twenty years, but the rents became ridiculous and he shut down the studio and built one at home. One of the reasons he made the switch to working from home a few years ago was he rarely saw his clients in the studio; everyone had already started to make the switch to remote. He has also done work with the DOD (Department of Defense) for nineteen years. He has never met the woman who is his main contact. He saw this work-from-home trend growing. No one wanted to drive to the studio when they could take care of things from home, especially not in L.A. For the past twelve years he has been at home. He says he never gets stuck in traffic anymore unless the dog is in front of him going down the stairs.

The downside of this for Nathan is he never really gets to leave work. He has no problem getting up at 5 AM for an East Coast studio gig, but when the East Coast signs off, he is still working. He works longer hours and he has issues with shutting the workday down. His biggest challenge is being able to network. Nathan finds that people find social media advertising less sincere and they do not always trust it. He would rather talk face-to-face. By his own admission he is a social animal. Connection is vital for him as an individual. He prefers the telephone because it is one-on-one and a more personal connection. His second favorite method of communication is email. He uses texting for short bursts of communication. He really is not into longer conversations on text. He would rather have a two-minute phone conversation than a fifteen-minute text. He really does not have a plan but realizes a plan might benefit him. He is certainly a connector and has no problem with reaching out. He is an early riser and finds he can get more done incredibly early. He says his industry has changed in the last five years. Technology has made the response time less and the urgency more immediate. People plan less and react more. He has done national commercials with less than an hour turnaround.

Nathan says his industry could support a remote workplace but was not ready. Before COVID-19, he was the exception rather than the rule by working from home. Most of the other voice talent does not or did not. Part of the challenge is getting actors to pay attention. This is amplified in the virtual world. He also finds that the demand for Non-Disclosure Agreements (NDAs) has drastically increased. Otherwise, there is relatively little compliance that he is aware of. A few years ago, working from home was mostly nonexistent. The norm was you came into the office and the studio. Agents want control. They have less control in the remote workplace. He finds that there is less understanding of privacy and non-disclosure with younger talent because they have always been online. The speed has also increased; now it is totally possible for talent to have a clip up and on YouTube in minutes. That is why NDAs have become so much more important.

He has all the equipment he needs. It is his business, and he has invested in it. He has a soundproof booth because, as Nathan stated, the neighbors do not care if you are working from home when they run the leaf blower. Because he is self-employed, he gets the tax benefits and invests wisely in what he needs. He has a secure upload site because he cannot just post information to public servers. Security is important with NDAs. Hardware, software and security can be challenging because of compatibility. Schedules can be tight. File sizes can be a challenge. Operating system compatibility and application updates can require workarounds. Files can be large and storage issues are mostly unaddressed. Without a major disaster, security is swept under the rug. No one really discusses it or addresses it.

On a scale of 1 to 4, 1 being I do not want to do this anymore and 4 I love it, Nathan would be a 4. He has been working from home for a long time and feels perfectly comfortable controlling his work environment. His partner is patient and, in his words, that is a good thing. Fortunately, she is retired; unfortunately he is on the phone and communicating all day. She had a very stress-filled job and has a lot of tolerance. Nathan tries to end his day by 5:30 or 6 PM so that he makes time for a personal and private life. He is a remarkably busy human and knows he needs downtime. He has free time. Does he have enough free time? He is not so sure.

Nathan is all about integrity. He thinks that online has a different energy for integrity. He blames this on the speed of connection. Integrity requires trust, and online can leave erroneous first impressions. He is concerned about his image and how quickly first impressions can be changed online. He feels like trolls and uncertainty can pop up out of nowhere and your online image can be changed. In Hollywood, integrity is hard to come by and when you compete for clients with all the other voiceover folks around the globe, your reputation is paramount. He has worked hard to maintain a separate private life. He also teaches classes and is dedicated to his students. Nathan works hard to set boundaries and he works at control. This is what helps with his comfort and success in the virtual environment.

He has seen his entire industry move to more of a gig economy style and that has drastically affected how and what people get paid. Everybody can work from home and everybody can talk and read so everyone thinks they can do voiceovers. Moving forward, he sees a very new normal and thinks it is important that things change. He sees the need for a dedicated space, being more able to define your work zone and the ability to set your own boundaries as keys to the new normal. Nathan sees the need for more structure in one's life because the world will be much less structured. He thinks this all was underway before COVID-19. He believes in having a plan and working the plan. Now, more than ever, we all need a plan, he says, an individual plan for our work and our lives. It is too easy to wander around aimlessly especially in this environment. He does not think face-to-face is going away. It is here to stay and the products will always exist in a face-to-face world but the way they get produced and how they get distributed, marketed and sold will all be done more and more virtually. Nathan believes that the face-to-face portion of every work process will shrink.

When I asked Nathan six months later, this is what he said: Nathan did not respond. Like many people, Nathan has gone missing temporarily. It happens a lot in the COVID-19 world. People are stressed, overwhelmed and unaccounted for.

Alex is in real estate. Actually, he is in real estate technology. He is an executive level manager for a global software company and provides software to property owners of low-income housing. He is a very bright guy. When I interviewed him in early April 2020, he explained that the company provides a full suite of software products including property management, accounting and other technologies. He is not a software engineer but rather an industry expert who understands the players and their needs. His professional life has spanned seventeen years and he has been working from home for a little less than a year. Before COVID-19, Alex spent a lot of time on airplanes. His job normally requires a great deal of travel. In his own words, "I'm a seasoned professional and I have built a lot of trust." He started working from home when he was promoted to a new job role. At his last job they actually had a policy where younger people who were new to the company could not work from home for a year or two until people got to know them and could trust that they would do their jobs. In his organization, remote work is linked directly to seniority, rank and trust. Trust is a big issue. Alex thinks that rank has a lot to do with it. He is an upper-level executive, and his job is to communicate, influence and implement strategy. Travel is just part of what he does. When he cannot travel, he has to be more creative, have a solid agenda and work harder at being an effective leader.

Alex always has a plan, but he is also is flexible. He has weekly one-on-ones with his boss, his direct reports, and his colleagues in different business units. He meets monthly with industry leaders. He calls it a cadence like a dance. He knows he has to talk to clients every day, and he needs to catch up with people who are not on his calendar and may not be scheduled. Some of his daily activities are planned and some come from a knowledge of what is important and what needs to get done. He can intuitively set and enact his priorities. Now, his entire company, about 1,700 people, are all working from home. A lot of the people in the company already had the way, the means and the methods to go remote.

His company was ready for this. Because they are a technology company, they have the equipment and the support they need to have a remote workforce. They are also an exceptionally large company and global, so they make it possible for people across all levels to access each other and do their jobs connecting with technologies. Much of the senior level leadership team already did not work at headquarters. The caveat is that normally these folks did a good bit of travel. Living on airplanes and in hotels was the norm.

They have to meet a lot of security and compliance standards because they are a software company, and they manage a lot of sensitive information. Every year they have to take tests to assure they know the standards but there is really no difference between someone working from home or in the office. It is a case of being aware and knowing what you are doing and what information you are working with and understanding the risks. The company provides the equipment, a VPN and a portal landing which secures entry into their systems and through their firewall. He uses his own phone and pays for his own internet services, but the company reimburses him.

Alex does a lot of work with housing authorities and these folks have been swamped because of COVID-19. They work with very vulnerable populations and the impact of this pandemic has been staggering. The company is busier than ever serving their clients who desperately need the technologies now more than ever. Fortunately, his organization was able to pull it together and transition to a global workplace fairly quickly and easily, partly because they were in the technology business. They had to figure it out fast but remote was not a big reach. They had a lot of the hardware and knowledge already. It was more a matter of organizing and coordinating the move to #WFH. The expectations of what the job requires and how people get that done were clear before everyone went remote.

The company uses Microsoft Teams and Alex finds it extremely helpful. You can automatically reach out to find people and connect with them. Because of the amount of travel these folks do, they use mobile devices quite often. They have email, review documents and hold synchronous meetings on their phones and they make good old-fashioned phone calls! He keeps two phones: one for company business and one for personal use.

He sees the remote workplace as the new trend and thinks there will be new lessons to learn. On a scale of 1 to 4, 1 being I do not want to do this anymore and 4 I love it, Alex would be a 4. He knows his job and takes responsibility for his role and achieving his goals. Being in a global technology business helps. He would be the first to tell you, though, that it is not for everyone and especially not for younger people with less workplace experience. It takes a while to adjust to the work world and trust is everything. He also understands that it does not replace all face-to-face connections. Once this COVID-19 pandemic is over, he expects to return to some travel, mostly because, in his opinion, it is necessary for influence, connection and getting results.

When I asked Alex six months later, this is what he said: My company has realized that the workforce can be very productive from home so they are deciding to permanently close offices around the country, including offices they never thought would be closed. I have mixed feelings about remote work. It's challenging because I'm an executive. It's hard to keep company morale high and motivate people virtually. However, since we're working remotely and have a travel ban until (at the earliest) 1/1/2021, I don't have a choice.

My company has absolutely supported me through this transition. For example, our large annual conference in October is now virtual. Instead of making me drive to another location to record my sessions, my company mailed me equipment so that I can participate in the conference from my home.

My job depends on air travel. Before the pandemic, I used to meet with my teams and our senior leadership team throughout the country periodically. I miss being able to nurture these relationships in person. Not being able to be around others means that other methods of communication have taken on a greater level of importance. Today, I write more, and I spend more time preparing for video conference calls so that I can overcompensate. I will be working from home for the foreseeable future. I wouldn't be surprised if I have to work from home until Q3 2021 or Q4 2021. Since I work in technology, an industry that is helping people stay connected during the pandemic, I don't expect for our company to suffer huge losses during this period.

However, we also depend on a vast network of real estate organizations which use our software including multi-family buildings, government-subsidized properties and corporate facilities. If the world continues to operate this way, our clients could experience economic pain which could ultimately impact us.

I think the lasting impact of the pandemic will be the dramatic decrease in travel and in person meetings, including client meetings and conferences. I also think that more of our employees will (more permanently) alter their homes to create permanent at-home workspaces. Many of us have created makeshift offices during this time but we may be forced to put more time and effort into permanent at-home office spaces.

As a company leader, I miss interacting with people in person, but my company has made working from home so easy that it's hard not to like it. Also, being in a tech company makes working from home manageable. If I had to pick a number, I would be a 3.

Matt   Matt is a high-level executive for a global technology firm. He is in a different industry but in a similar role to Alex. When I interviewed him in early April 2020, he had been working remotely for years. His company is in digital learning and data analytics. They are a technology company at heart and the business is workplace learning. Prior to COVID-19, he worked from home most of the time and went into his Manhattan office maybe once a week. It is the nature of the business and working from home was nothing new for Matt. Their clients are multinational organizations, located all over the globe. Matt loves working from home. He cannot imagine anything else. He has a two-year-old and cannot imagine not being there to see his son growing up. He finds it to be a major benefit of working for his organization.

One of Matt's biggest challenges is shutting the workday down. The workday tends to get away from him working from home. He can start the day at 7 or 8 AM and find himself working at 8 PM pretty regularly. It is hard to shut it off, especially when his office is in New York and headquarters is located several continents, oceans, and time zones away. The nine to five day just doesn't work for him. He loves his job but still finds it necessary to turn it off for personal sanity. This is complicated by his clients, which tend to be larger organizations and traditionally face-to-face based. Even though most of them are working from home with COVID-19, there is still a requirement for regular office hours. The familiar, traditional comfort zone established in the workplace as a 9 to 5 routine is hard to disrupt.

They work with medical companies, aviation and others where most of the training is compliance training. Many of these organizations still believe face-to-face classroom training with instructor-directed learning is "king." Addressing the internal politics and issues unique to each organizational culture can make a difference in business. Remote can create some challenges in efficiency and connection for people who are not constantly working in this kind of office.

Matt's company was ready for this and they were already doing it. COVID did not create a different workday. It did not impact client relationships that much, especially on his side of the fence. Many of his clients had already discovered remote training because of the cost involved with flying people to headquarters. E-learning was a much more effective, trackable and a lower cost alternative to the traditional classroom. Their technology allows them to customize learning solutions based on experience and software interfaces. They analyze data from desktops, machines and events, and then create customized solutions for the individual. Their mission is to remove silos through the use of data. Welcome to the twenty-first century; they are not alone. He finds that many of his clients are supported working from home as much as they want to be; some just prefer the office.

Matt's role is relationship-driven and he is in charge of business development. Networking and opening channels of communication and connection is basically what he does. He doesn't get into the nitty gritty of the technology or the training design. He really doesn't have a structure for communication other than a few regularly scheduled monthly meetings. They use real time tools like Slack and try to respond quickly and remain nimble. Most of the planning is client-centered. He checks his emails and goes from there.

His company brings the digital perspective. He sees the world changing. Many compliance issues can't be addressed in a face-to-face environment anymore, so companies have to adjust. Matt thinks it is a transition that is long overdue. Many rules are written for a work environment that no longer serves the organizations. The way they function has to change. He sees the speed of change increasing and compliance addressing a new norm. His firm is governed by his clients' compliance issues. The company's biggest concerns are data security issues. His biggest issue is compatibility with networks and technologies. But generally, it's not a big deal because he works for a technology company.

They use a lot of AWS (Amazon Web Services) and IBM. The company is fairly flat and definitely global. They have always been global. The majority of folks live in New Zealand. Everything they create is mobile-ready and usable across platforms, or at least that is what they strive for: desktop, phones and tablets. They use whatever their clients use. They try to be nimble. Everything is on Slack. Productivity is measured in terms of ROI (return on investment).

On a scale of 1 to 4, 1 being I do not want to do this anymore and 4 I love it, Matt is a 4. He's been a 4 for a long time. He loves working from home and wouldn't want to change it. This COVID-19 pandemic didn't change his workday or workplace; it was just another day in the office. He loves the ten-step commute. He appreciates being at home with his family and understands blending not blurring work and having a private life. He has adjusted to working with the international time differences and uses his schedule wisely. He is flexible with his time but realistic. He thinks that both time management and the comfort level working from home is determined by the industry and the age of the worker. As Matt points out, his generation has always had the digital connection and the technology industry is more flexible in many ways than most.

Moving forward, Matt suggests it is imperative we embrace the changes that are in front of us. Our work environments are changing, and that change will continue. It's important to embrace it and use it to your benefit. If it's a pandemic today, it might be AI tomorrow. Matt says you have a choice: You can either resent the change or embrace it and figure out where you fit in. For Matt, attitude is everything. He says, embrace the "new normal" and manage your attitude. Make the most of the opportunities the remote workplace presents, both professionally and personally. Finally, make the effort to connect and reach out to others. Matt admits this environment requires a little more effort to connect both professionally and personally.

When I asked Matt six months later, this is what he said: Matt did not return my emails or phone calls. I suspect he has had his hands full with clients trying to adapt to a new workplace. I see him regularly and he is doing well. He is just extremely busy!

Chapter 12

Just Another Day at the Office

U.S. workers who are being asked to return to the office six months after the pandemic sent them home are saying "no so fast." Most would rather work from home at least a few days a week. Not that they don't miss the office and their colleagues but more that they really like #WFH. The once familiar office routine has been interrupted by being able to work from home. No more dry-cleaning bills, dressing up or commuting. They get more done even if they are working in the backyard on the deck, at the kitchen counter or in their bedrooms. Surveys by PricewaterhouseCoopers in June 2020 found that nearly 33% of their workers would prefer to never have to return to the office and 72% said they wanted to work from home at least two days a week. Two months later in August, Wells Fargo/Gallup found that 42% liked working from home and only 14% viewed it negatively.

Companies are encouraging and some are commanding workers to return to the office. Many workers are saying "not so fast." Some of this reticence might be around healthcare issues, but most of it is because they have discovered a better way to work and love it. Nearly 66% say they are more productive at home, even with disruptions and a few challenges. Most say they can get twice as much done in half the time. And no one misses the commute.

Older workers, 65 and above, have a much less likely chance of working from home. Economic disparities and COVID have made it difficult for them to work and policy makers have done little to help. Many older workers have had to quit their jobs, and few have received relief, especially longer term. Nearly 5 million older workers in the pandemic economy were not able to work from home. This is the same population that is at higher risk for contracting COVID. The CDC reported that originally 8 out of 10 deaths from the pandemic were in adults 65 or older, and a significant number found themselves in intensive care units and required hospitalization. Many people in this population were the first to be let go while some will continue to go to work because they have to. Many workers younger and older than 65 will continue going to work and potentially risking their health and that of their families.

Less than one in five black workers and roughly one in six Hispanic workers are able to work from home. They are essential workers, production workers and low wage workers. These folks are much less likely to be able to work remotely than higher-wage and white-collar workers. Younger workers, ages fifteen to twenty-four, are the least likely to be able to work from home. This is not surprising when you consider the types of jobs these populations commonly hold.

Remote schooling has had a vastly different response. Most schools did not have a strategic plan and what resulted was huge amounts of stress. This directly affects working parents and their ability to juggle work and family in the work-from-home environment. It makes it difficult for parents to figure out how they are going to manage everything, whether they are at home or in the office, and it is incredibly stressful. Most though still prefer working at home because it quiets the internal debate over not being close enough and not being able to juggle family and work. But many parents, particularly single and lower-income families, are experiencing a catastrophe firsthand.

Schools rushed to get Chromebooks into students' hands and make Internet hotspots available but there was little or no training for teachers. Online teaching requires training, planning and time to be executed well. Some people are lucky enough to have grandparents who can help out, or the money to hire a full-time nanny or tutor, but this is not true for everybody. Working parents have taken on an additional burden, that of homeschooling. They now have three full time jobs: parent, teacher and employee. Most parents are doing their best but have never been trained in teaching and know little about tutoring their children. They are also under significant financial strains and remarkable stress levels. Many people have been furloughed or laid off and this just increases the stress. Probably what is the most shocking is what it has revealed about our school systems. Their autonomy has created a situation where state governments cannot and will not step in to have any creative or even plausible solutions. Both the short- and long-term impact on children, teachers and the economy, not to mention on learning, are incalculable. Because of the length of the pandemic, many people have had to return to work, only to be sent home again. Their children may or may not be back in school, remote, hybrid or face-to-face, and quite often this is changing daily.

We've also learned that our schools and teachers do a lot more than teach a curriculum. They function as babysitters, counselors, and provide a social setting that is critical to the development of children. All this was lost when we went remote because we had no plan. Many working parents have had to choose to stay home and have lost their livelihood, insurance, and employment because they did not have alternative childcare options. Teachers are supposed to magically know how to teach online using synchronous platforms like Zoom and Google. There is no plan, and with multiple children comes multiple interfaces, technologies and more confusion. For parents it is often an impossible situation, for the teachers is it is completely impossible. K-12 is a mess, and the losses and impact will affect this generation for a long time.

Higher Education is not in much better shape. Enrollments are plummeting and a sector of the economy that has resisted the integration of technologies and online learning for decades all of a sudden decided to go remote. Colleges and universities need to understand that the autonomy of faculty, intellectual property and excuses are not a reason to confuse emergency remote teaching (ERT) with good online learning. Many have responded to this public health crisis by cancelling face-to-face classes, and those that haven't probably wish they had. In Washington D.C., one out of four COVID-19 cases originates on a college campus. Institutions of all sizes and types—Ivy League, state schools and community colleges—literally hundreds of institutions have moved online overnight. The speed of this transition is staggering and unprecedented and impossible. Although college technical support staff is trying, enabling this kind of transition in such a short window of time is absurd. Good online learning takes planning, knowledge and commitment to quality. The temptation to compare this ridiculous attempt to suddenly adapt a delivery mode that has been resisted by faculty for decades mostly due to ignorance is political at best. The teaching and learning solutions being generated online vary greatly and the results are tenuous.

Enough with the criticism of online learning. Research has supported it is equal to if not better than face-to-face learning in many content areas. A hurried attempt to move curriculum online under these circumstances will not take advantage of the affordances of technologies and the possibilities of the online format. Even with minimal training, most faculty will not understand the important differences that the professionals in instructional design and educational technology have researched and understood for decades. Higher Education is likely to criticize online while it waits for a return to "normal."

What is being delivered in most cases is emergency teaching, not online learning, and there is an extraordinarily strong distinction in these terms. Online learning has been studied in detail for decades and the quality of the instructional design makes all the difference. To promote social distancing during the pandemic everybody rushed to online. Many institutions both in K-12 and Higher Education have resisted the integration of online technologies for a variety of reasons, usually justifying it by the erroneous assumption that online is of lower quality. The inequalities of our educational system across the board have been exposed.

The "new normal" for education, both K-12 and Higher Education, will include more blended learning, more hybrid instruction and certainly more technology. What is desperately needed is a plan. A plan that utilizes research and optimizes what technology has to offer in a learning environment. Typical online planning and delivery of a university level course takes six to nine months. It takes an investment of money, resources and time, and a strong instructional plan to achieve optimal results. Evaluations of what has taken place in ERT may give colleges and universities and K-12 a peek at possibilities for online delivery and optimizing hybrid instruction, but that's it. What this crisis has really done is point out the need to modernize our educational systems. It has disrupted students, staff, faculty, parents and the core of what we call education. The pandemic has presented unique challenges, and everybody has done their best to meet them. Moving forward it is time to face these challenges and develop a plan to do better.

The COVID-19 pandemic has disrupted the way organizations work. This was no small move. The transition was abrupt, and the social and emotional confusion has left long lasting effects on the global population. Organizations find themselves fully physically dispersed, relying entirely on digital communications and technologies to do their jobs. Prior to this time many people who worked from home did so with the help of a full-time office staff in the physical office. Prior to COVID-19 most remote work was voluntary and formal. #WFH agreements were rare. Patterns of digital communication have changed and the walk down the hall is now a Zoom meeting or a text message. The total number of meetings per day has gone up by almost 13% and more people are in the meetings, but they are shorter. There are many more emails and the number of people copied on each email has also increased. However, the longer the pandemic goes on, the number of cc's and text messages seems to be leveling out a bit.

The National Bureau of Economic Research in Cambridge, MA conducted a study that digs deeply into communication patterns and how they changed in 2020. What they found was that the COVID-19 shutdown forced people to communicate more effectively. We adapted very quickly and actually began to change our communication patterns even before the official shutdowns. Employees and employers adapted their work schedules and extended the range of time they were available to work. There was an overarching increase in virtual communications, but this is not surprising. We are working longer hours and the workday extends well beyond traditional working hours. No conclusion was drawn as to whether the longer workday is beneficial or a detrimental to employee well-being.

Across the board, from the classroom to the firehouse to Big Oil to Hollywood, we moved out of the office. As it turns out, most people don't miss it. The results of the New York Times and Morning Consult study published on August 23, 2020 indicated that out of 1,123 people surveyed, 86% said they were satisfied with their current working arrangement. Although it took some getting used to, working from bedrooms and closets and in pajamas, people adapted. No one misses the commute and people are getting more exercise, walking and getting outside more. It's much less stressful than sitting in traffic and much more productive than they imagined. There is less gossip and lower, if any, dry cleaning bills. Different people adapt to change differently and "life still happens." The COVID-19 crisis has given us all an opportunity to change how we work once and for all.

What We Learned   There is near unanimous agreement that working from home can be a positive experience. People need people and face-to-face contact is important for connection but working online is possible and can be highly productive. Most states and most companies do not have a remote work policy for things like subsidies, compliance and security. Maybe because they are the home to so many tech companies, California is the exception. We were not ready for the remote workplace. Many companies still had localized systems and lacked a consistent approach. The ones that had a company firewall portal and cloud-based access to systems and resources had the easiest time with the transition. This is where employees can sign on from the office or the bedroom using dual authentication, and once they are in the systems, they can be anywhere; the interface and access is the same.

Working from home is more productive and easier to execute than many expected. The issues of trust, for the most part, were cultural and ill-founded. People want to do a good job and just need some training in productivity and engagement online. They need emotional connections, clear expectations from their leaders and tips on how to work from home comfortably. They need boundaries for time and the flexibility to limit their cognitive load including children, pets, and the office environment. They want time to take care of their kids, exercise and get off of the screen. The remote workplace can be full of distractions and without a structure and routine it can become overwhelming. People need connection and they need to be recognized as individuals and feel important. They want to belong. They want to communicate and have clear guidance. They want to be listened to. The transition to working from home requires patience from both the employer and the employees.

Work from home is here to stay. The technology to do this effectively is here and getting better every day. Hybrid is the preferred option for many people, giving them the opportunity to connect and be together. They spend a few days in the office and a few days at home. There is a learning curve for #WFH. It takes time to adapt and realize how to be productive and to stay healthy and mentally sound. Also, to be secure and productive, it's important to have a dedicated and private space and a schedule to follow. Routine is important in the work from home environment.

Online learning in the corporate environment, K-12, and Higher Education is here to stay and will continue to grow. Many companies are planning on staying remote after the pandemic crisis is over. Why? Money. On average working online saves companies a lot of money. As I state in The Pajama Effect, it saves about $23,000 per year per employee. That's huge. Schools are discovering these savings and the "new normal" will look much different than the world we once knew. Employees are also saving money on gasoline, parking and childcare. Pollution and carbon admissions are going down. The air is getting cleaner and it's easier to breathe. What will happen to the leasing agent's business and office space? No one really knows.

Phone calls are back in style. It's important to connect one-on-one and not just with text messages. The verbal cues of phone calls and person-to-person connections make picking up the phone and making that call more important than ever. Sometimes it makes all the difference.

We need policy, new legal strategies and compliance structures both internally in organizations and on a state and federal level. Employment law needs to change to reflect the relevance and importance of safety and security in the remote environment. Things like reimbursement and provisions for software and hardware need to be in writing. Human Resources needs to play a much bigger role in providing and specifying what is acceptable in the remote work environment. The future of work is changing and training (in virtual project management, collaboration, video conferencing, asynchronous tools like Teams and Slack) is paramount. We need to focus learning and development initiatives on setting objectives, giving clear and positive feedback, recognizing the individual and on how we learn online. This is not a future that is coming, it is a future that has arrived. Thanks to COVID-19 and our emergency rush to social distance, work from home (#WFH) is here and is here to stay. Now it is time to stop the discussions of whether it is possible or not and accept that it is. Now it is time to create innovations and design a workplace that optimally supports #WFH... working and learning from home.

References and Resources

BBC Worklife (2020) How COVID-19 led to a nationwide work-from-home experiment. Retrieved from https://www.bbc.com/worklife/article/20200309-coronavirus-COVID-19-advice-chinas-work-at-home-experiment

Bennett, J. and Strzemein, A. (2020) Out of the Office. New York Times, Sunday August 23, 2020.

Bersin, J. (2020) Remote Work Is Sinking In: And the Impact is Bigger Than We Realized. May 6, 2020

DeFilppis, E., Impink, S.M., Polzer, J., Sadum, R. and Singell, M. (2020) Collaborating During the Coronavirus: The Impact of COVID-19 On the Nature of Work. National Bureau of Economic Research, Cambridge Mass. July 2020.

Gelles, D. (2020) *When a Home Becomes Headquarters*. The Corner Office. New York Times, March 29, 2020.

Gelles, D. (2020) You Can Take Your Job Home with You. The Corner Office. New York Times, July 19, 2020.

Gould, E. (2020) *Older Workers Can't Work from Home and Are at Higher Risk for COVID-19*. Economic Policy Institute. Working Economics Blog. March 31, 2020.

Hechinger, J. and Lorin, J. (2020) *Ready or Not Colleges Go Online*. Bloomberg Businessweek. Ellis, James Ellis Ed.. March 23, 2020

Hodges, C., Moore, S., Lockee, B., Trust, T., and Bond, A. (2020) The Difference Between Emergency Remote Teaching and Online Learning. March 27, 2020. frankie's/Shutterstock.com

Meister, J. (2020). The Impact of The Coronavirus on HR And The New Normal Of Work. Retrieved from https://www.forbes.com/sites/jeannemeister/2020/03/31/the-impact-of-the-coronavirus-on-hr-and-the-new-normal-of-work/?utm_campaign=Care%40

Perlman, D. (2020) *The COVID-19 Parent Trap*. New York Times, Sunday July 5, 2020.

Shapiro, S., Bazelon, E., Chung, N., Tough, P. (2020) The Education Issue. The Lost Year. The New York Times Magazine, September 13, 2020.

Tinder, B. (2020) The Impact of COVID-19 on HR & HR Technology-Related Projects. The Raven Insight. May 4, 2020. Ravenintel.com

The Washington Post (2020) Facebook, Google, Microsoft say most workers will work from home until 2021. Retrieved from https://www.washingtonpost.com/technology/2020/05/18/facebook-google-work-from-home/ 1/10

#WFH
Interview Questions

1. What is your job? What industry are you in? What do you do?

2. What is your general reaction to working from home? Do you feel comfortable? Have you done it before?

3. What are the biggest challenges?

4. How do you interact with people? Do you have a plan? What does your daily schedule look like?

5. In your opinion was your company/organization ready for the remote workplace? Do they support you working from home?

6. Are you aware of any compliance legal issues in the remote workplace unique to your situation?

7. Do you have the equipment/software and access you need to get your job done? Do you employees? Who supplies it? Do you use mobile platforms?

8. How do you meet your job requirements? Are the expectations clear? Does your boss feel comfortable with you working from home?

9. What difficulties have you experienced with hardware/software/security?

10. How do you like working from home? 1 to 4

11. How does it impact your family life? Personal affairs? Free time? Is it more flexible?

12. What suggestions do you have for moving forward working in a remote environment?

#WFH
Questions Six Months Later

It's six months later...

1. What are the long-term implications of remote work that you see now (that maybe you didn't see last spring)? Where are you now and where is it going?

2. How do you feel about the loss of in-person contact with your teammates and clients?

3. Has your company continued to support you all the way through this so far?

4. What do you miss most about life prior to March 2020 (or when we shut down)?

5. What does your job look like now for the rest of 2020 and 2021?

6. How do you think the pandemic will alter the future of your work?

7. On a scale of 1 to 4 (1 you do not like WFH and 4 you love it) where would you be now? Pick a number.

*All participants signed a non-disclosure agreement and their names have been changed for their employment protection.

The Pajama Effect

Success Skills for Working and Leading in a Virtual Environment

Excerpt

> Work spotlights the character of people: some turn up their sleeves, some turn up their noses, and some don't turn up at all.
> —Sam Ewing

Chapter 1

Why Go to the Office?

Over the course of a year, 50 million people worldwide will begin the day by waking up in the morning, pouring a cup of enthusiasm and then walking into their offices in pajamas or whatever suits them.

Whether that "office" is the kitchen table, the basement or a hotel room, these individuals experience unique benefits – but not without challenges. Take Kelly, for example, who enjoys the flexibility of working from home because she has a small child. Yet, on any given day, you may find Kelly simultaneously doing the laundry, chasing her 3-year-old and typing a report, all while she waits for a scheduled web conference to begin. Then there is Robert, who used to get up at 4 a.m. to beat traffic and make it to the office on time. His new job is remote but requires that he collaborate with his teammates on a regular basis. His teammates, however, don't live on the same continent; one is in Madrid and the other one in Beijing. Both Kelly and Robert cannot successfully perform their jobs unless they make mental and physical shifts.

The term "workshifting" is used to describe what happens when people find themselves working out of trains, hotel lobbies or from their kitchen tables (Lister & Harnish, 2010). The idea of working or going to school in your pajamas is not a new concept.

There are plenty of ads out there highlighting the advantages of working or learning through digitally mediated tools. Among the advantages portrayed: staying in your pajamas or, at least, not having to wear business attire. Currently, there is increased interest in working virtually because organizations now rely on technology to do more with less.

The Pajama Effect, however, is more than changing your work location from the traditional office space to a corner of your home or hotel room. *The Pajama Effect* is a state of being where you find yourself out of your element and where normal constraints and boundaries no longer apply. *The Pajama Effect* involves a psychological and then behavioral shift. To function best in this dramatically different environment, you must focus on what it takes to be successful in the virtual world. This new workplace wilderness is an environment that is physically detached, where the conventional structure of the workplace has vanished. Interruptions and distractions abound, making it difficult to get the job done.

The Pajama Effect is a phenomenon brought about by the breaking down of walls. This absence of tradition and structure creates flexibility and new responsibilities affecting every facet of personal and professional life. Smartphones and digital communications have changed the 9-to-5 workday to a 24/7/365 never-ending cycle. You find yourself answering work emails while watching your child's baseball game or texting your friend during an Internet-based business conference. There are more demands placed on your time than ever before and instant responses are expected. *The Pajama Effect* helps you understand what it takes to function successfully as you work in this detached yet highly connected and demanding world.

How did we get here? It all happened very fast, and there are no signs of it slowing down. For example, the story you may read today goes viral within 24 hours but then, within another 24 hours or less, it is considered old news. New fortunes are made and reputations are destroyed overnight. There is no time for psychological gestation or conscious absorption before we are on to the next thing. The pace at which we live is continually becoming faster.

It is important to understand how we got here in order to see where we are headed. Let's take a trip down memory lane, back to the year 1999. That certainly was a big year; it may have been the year of biggest change. Situated at the dawn of the 21st century, in 1999, we were surrounded by exciting technological advancements yet many of us went to the office wearing a suit and faithfully following a 9-to-5 routine. We did not realize the potential of these advancements. In the meantime, programmers around the globe scrambled to make sure 1999 could turn into the year 2000 and the earth would keep on spinning. (Remember the fears about Y2K?) Even after all the 9s safely became 0s, some of us were partying like it was 1999 because we did not fully understand how technology was affecting our lives. Radical and dramatic changes had already begun.

The year 2000 doesn't seem that long ago. Mark Zuckerberg, founder of Facebook, was in high school. Google was an infant corporation and Microsoft was the evil empire. There was no iPad, no

Emergence of the Virtual Office

iPod and no iTunes. We had Learning Management Systems, but Web 2.0 was only a buzzword and the presidential election depended on counting votes on punch-style paper ballots. As we moved to a 3G network, connectivity increased, as did outsourcing and the use of digitally mediated communications. The barriers of time and place were slowly but permanently being blurred, affecting individuals, organizations and society at large.

The impact of these technological advancements is evident in the swift economic changes that now affect how you earn a living, especially as the economic position of the United States on the world stage has changed drastically. With the dollar value plummeting, only 36 percent of the top 500 global companies are now U.S.-based. China, the sleeping giant, has awakened and taken the lead in many areas of commerce. Brazil, Russia, India and China (known as the BRIC countries) are some of the fastest growing economies in the world. These, by the way, are the same countries to which the U.S. outsourced manufacturing, technology, accounting and production jobs not so long ago. The outsourcing trend altered western economies, making them no longer based on the production of goods or services. As a result, these economies evolved to include the "knowledge worker" (Lesonsky, 2011) as a key player in a company's success.

The term "knowledge worker" originally meant one who works primarily with information or who develops or uses knowledge in the workplace. In today's workplace, it commonly describes individuals who are experts in a certain subject area.

For a brief moment in time, it seemed that knowledge workers were not part of the outsourcing trend. Then technology caused the world to shrink, opening previously unforeseen possibilities. Knowledge workers in remote locations emerged. The lines between knowledge and information blurred, but both became available without anyone having to leave home.

Today, information and expertise are shared in nanoseconds, regardless of geographic locations or time zones. Whether it is the outsourced doctor in a remote country who reviews your child's x-ray while you wait at your local emergency room, or the programmers in India who write the code that runs the New York Stock Exchange, knowledge is shared around the globe. Many positions are staffed from the global labor market and many jobs today require virtual teaming and collaboration. This new type of worker is not bound by traditional office rules. Today's worker has the challenge of adapting to the demands of the virtual office. Digital connectivity has made knowledge a temporary thing, because new knowledge is generated constantly. Even new products and ideas are quickly outdated because someone else across the globe builds and creates a new product or idea. As Bill Gates reportedly once put it, "Intellectual property has the shelf life of a banana."

The changes affecting our global workforce are broader in scope than just the change from factory worker to knowledge worker. Because we have gone from stationary to mobile and from analog to digital, the make-up of the global workforce has rapidly changed. Many baby boomers and digital immigrants now find themselves out of jobs, struggling to go back into a job market dominated by technology. Digital immigrants by definition are all the folks who were born before the PC age, even if they owned the original Atari or played Pac-Man or Pong. Unless they update their skills, these digital immigrants stand no chance when competing in the job market with digital natives, who were born surrounded by electronic technology. Digital natives work online, they live online and they socialize online. They expect technologies to be part of how they live, work and play. They do not know life without digital connectivity.

Even though the majority of workers today still work in a traditional office, more people find themselves workshifting. In 1995, when author and computer expert Woody Leonhard wrote, "Work is something you do, not something you travel to," he probably realized that what affects the bottom line of a business is that the job gets done, regardless of location. The terms "telecommuting" and "telecommute" were first used by University of Southern California researcher Jack Nilles in 1973. Today, telecommuters may work from home a few hours per week or the entire week. If you are one of them, you may or may not work in your pajamas and you may or may not have to collaborate with someone in a different time zone, but the effect is the same. You are working remotely and you live by connecting in the virtual environment.

In this book, the terms "virtual worker' and "pajama worker" are used interchangeably to mean a person who uses technologies to work, play or learn virtually. The terms "virtual office" and "virtual workplace" are used interchangeably to describe where the virtual worker "works."

The virtual environment is very different from that of a traditional office. You are not in a physical location provided for and directly controlled by your employer. As a virtual worker, you work from home, on the train, at coffee shops, airports and soccer games. You use text, chat, conference calls and virtual meeting applications. Your daily commute to a physical location is replaced by technologies. All of these changes affect the way you work, play and learn.

"Virtual" means that people are functioning in cyberspace in one way or another. You live, work and play in a world connected by digital communications that does not require you to meet face to face in order to conduct business or maintain social relationships. In the virtual environment, you are detached physically but connected by technologies. Society at large has been transformed by the new methods of communication. Now there are critical behavioral components necessary for success in this digitally connected environment.

The emergence of the virtual office is an inevitable byproduct of these technologies. Some see the emergence of the virtual office as annoying, scary or even as an unacceptable way of doing business. Others embrace it as a "growing pain" that companies must experience in order to survive tough economic times and forge new markets in a global economy. Bottom line: Organizations that do not embrace the change will sooner or later be swept under by it.

Because the global economic infrastructure is so interconnected, dramatic changes in the way we work have spread rapidly regardless of the industry. Businesses that fail to adapt to the changes brought about by technology will find themselves unable to compete in the global marketplace, making their products and services either outdated or obsolete altogether. The traditional office is no longer able to support the needs of postindustrial economies, and it certainly cannot sustain the development of innovative new business models.

Before the digital age, the business landscape included defined roles, time boundaries and explicit face-to-face communication. Companies found it challenging to find qualified employees from a limited geographical pool of applicants. The emphasis was more on a firm handshake than on the ability to build trust through a well-written email. Today, however, the employee enjoys more flexibility but also more responsibility. The workday is fluid yet it merges with personal time, often blurring the lines between both. Communication today is woven and integrated into every aspect of the workday. This communication is more abstract, contextual, text-based, qualitative and emotional than ever before. Companies expect their employees to be able to seal the deal, no handshake needed; an email or a recorded video conversation will do.

What does the new workplace look like? It looks like wherever you are – your dinner table, home office or hotel room. Its quality is influenced by the technology you use, the social conditions you are in and the productivity stress you are under. It takes the form of the nature of the work you do, and the pressures and the challenges you face. It takes on the inexorable traits of human nature. You may be working on the road, in your basement, in an automobile or on a plane; you may have a 24/7/365 workweek. This new workplace is without the limits and boundaries you took for granted in the old office. It is ubiquitous. It is everywhere, ever-present and always turned on. It makes demands on you that the human psyche was not made for.

The virtual workplace has distinctive traits that are very different than most traditional office environments. The virtual office is characterized by openness, vulnerability, personal privacy, informality and detachment. It must be open, flexible and grounded on a common business vision.

Characteristics of the Virtual Office

This means that the virtual office is never really closed, yet its hours of operation are flexible. We check our email on the go via our favorite gadget and we can reply from the gym or the dentist's office. To be open also means that we must be open to new ideas and new ways of doing things. We cannot rely on old habits or old configurations. Success depends on relationships grounded in a common business vision and working together toward a common goal. Just as in the traditional office, only more so, if a team member does not believe in the overall mission, the rest of the team will feel the burden and have to pick up the slack. The virtual office gives you more and easier places to hide, escape and make excuses. Lack of contribution will eventually diminish trust as well as the power of collaboration.

Management of virtual workers requires expectations that are clearly stated and adhered to. As you may already know, organizational culture depends on the perceptions of its members. If the stakeholders distrust leadership, the organizational culture will suffer. The organizational leadership is ultimately responsible for uniting the virtual workers under a common vision. Sometimes this can be very difficult, especially if the virtual worker is more open and flexible than the leaders. There needs to be a balance between openness, flexibility and the cohesiveness of the team. You may be able to march to the beat of your own drum, but eventually you must also be able to join the band.

In the virtual workplace, you are very vulnerable to change. You must expect the unexpected. Change is the only constant. You will be in a state of perpetual motion unless you learn how to stop and breathe. There will always be something new to learn, whether it is how to use a new technology tool, develop a new strategy or acquire a new skill. Change also comes from your ever-evolving priorities. Very often you will find yourself moving, changing or shifting – not only office locations, but work and life priorities, responsibilities and connections.

The flexibility inherent in the virtual office provides you with more personal choices. If something goes wrong, you simply change your approach. Sometimes you will have time to reflect on the situation, but other times you will be hard-pressed to trust your gut and make an instant decision. The pajama worker has more personal privacy than the person working in the traditional office. Some of the expressions of this privacy may be obvious, such as working in your PJs because you haven't gotten dressed yet or in your bikini so you can work on your tan. Other reasons are less explicit, like finally being able to go with your child on a school field trip, or hiding from the world – unshaven and wearing the same shirt – until the project is finished. The point is, when you shift from a traditional office to a virtual one, you will feel a new sense of personal privacy within your physical world.

The demand for aligning your connections will force you to come out of your cave and join the other virtual inhabitants. You will be expected to collaborate across boundaries of time, space and disciplines. You will be expected to contribute your expertise but also synthesize and evaluate the contributions of others and make decisions that are best for the task you have been entrusted to complete. You will often feel like a fish out of water, trying to understand the perspectives of those from other cultural backgrounds. You are also likely to be placed in a team of individuals you have never met before, and have no idea if they can be trusted.

The virtual office is highly informal but results-oriented. There is no dress code and no official lunch break. You must determine what works for you and how you will handle interruptions. Who will get the door if you are on the phone with a client? How will your spouse notify you if the toilet leaks? Who will take care of the barking dog during your web conference? These are all informal but important protocols. They are rules you must establish in your household, because no one wants to hear your barking pooch when they are trying to participate in a webinar. Such interruptions also give the impression that you are unprofessional and informality should not be confused with unprofessionalism. Everyone loves babies, but when they are crying in the background it is impossible to get the job done. The virtual office is not a way to hide out and escape the business world.

Informality should have no direct impact on the end results. In the virtual office, you want to focus on the goal and use project management techniques to track your own progress. You want to learn to measure how your energies are spent and where the time is going. The responsibility to get the job done rests with you and no one else. As a pajama worker, you are responsible for seeking help when needed and tapping into the right resources to maximize your productivity. This is definitely a results-oriented environment (Gregory, 2010).

Finally, the virtual office is geographically detached but you are always able to be connected. You may have to get up earlier than expected or stay up five extra hours in order to speak to a virtual colleague or client who is in a different time zone. Your device may beep while you are in the shower and instead of reaching for the towel, you reach for the phone. Low and behold, it's the purchase order you were hoping for. All is well. This scene is not too different from what is now known as the "smartphone prayer." The phrase is used to describe the physical stance people take when secretly working on their smartphones during face-to-face meetings, in airports or restaurants, on dates, at the ball game, and pretty much everywhere they feel the urge to "check in": they carefully hold the phone with both hands, head bowed, quietly but intently typing on the screen. There is always more room for improvement, however, as someone posted on a blog, "The smartphone prayer is a plea to God to abolish the damn things."

In the virtual workplace, you want to be able to respond to the pressures of this new way of life. Such pressures are constant and they come from all angles. The verb "respond" evokes counter action of some sort, which is exactly what is needed in this environment to not only get the job done, but also to stay afloat in a sea of professional and personal demands. The technology beckons you to stay connected; it "trains" you to provide and to expect feedback. As a result, you create new habits, some good and some detrimental to your success. Each message you receive reinforces your response to "check in."

Our ability to respond to this stress can and will make or break your success on the digital frontier. Just like the explorers and industrialists needed skills that matched their time in history, the virtual worker needs certain abilities to thrive. There are five essential *respond-abilities* needed to thrive in the digital jungle: 1) act with autonomy, 2) set and enact priorities, 3) be authentically productive, 4) make responsible choices, and 5) align connections. Later in the book, we will explore these respond-abilities in more detail and learn how as individuals we can develop responses that are advantageous.

The emergence of the virtual office has pushed dramatic changes upon us all. For right now, let's reflect on the following point: It is the characteristics of the virtual office – openness, vulnerability, personal privacy, informality and detachment – that compel us to learn new behaviors in order to cope with challenges and flourish in this environment. It is essential that you learn how these characteristics affect you, personally and professionally. You also want to understand what the consequences of all these changes may be. Only then will you be able to acclimate yourself to the new environment and achieve success.

The pace at which we communicate has increased and so has the physical distance. Yet the technology tools we use to communicate make the increased physical distance a non-issue. You are expected to do more in less time, process more information faster and remain connected with practically no "off" time. Pajama workers behave in different ways and react differently because they are under different workplace stressors. In the virtual work environment, the practice of deliberately responding and not reacting is paramount.

Why Would You Want to Work Virtually?

You may choose to become a virtual worker or your company may simply send you home to work. Either way, you should be aware of some of the pros and cons for both you and your employer. After all, there are two sides to every coin. Advantages of the virtual workplace definitely outweigh the disadvantages for your employer, and it can be the same for you. First, working in the virtual office saves relocation time and travel costs, for both you and your employer. Second, productivity tends to be greater and development times shorter. Finally, it is obviously a convenient commute.

The new workplace is more responsive to connection and likely to increase a company's knowledge base because remote employees must share their knowledge with team members to get the job done. This new environment values creativity, self-assessment, reflection, and high performance standards. The pajama worker must be able to problem-solve and make critical decisions. Companies can also access the best resources, including talent, at the cheapest prices, keeping costs down. Individuals working remotely often feel a greater degree of freedom, personal privacy and autonomy. Leadership can organize teams along functional lines or cross-functional lines according to need, without being concerned about each individual's physical location. Organizations have an unprecedented level of flexibility, cohesiveness and connection. Both product development and commercialization can be achieved from the virtual office.

There are also a few disadvantages to the new workplace. Interaction must be intentional rather than accidental because there is a lack of physical contact. You will no longer run into the boss or a colleague in the break room; you will no longer be able to walk by your colleague's desk and discuss the next project. Things by necessity are done in a more intentional and structured way but may not require the same level of formality, which may sound like an oxymoron. The virtual workplace defies traditional power structures and minimizes formal protocols. For example, if you have a question, you have to seek out someone who has the knowledge you need. This can be achieved via a phone call, an instant message or a text message. The entire Internet is your knowledge base and you don't have to wait for the next meeting to get the information you need. You generally do not wait to speak to your supervisor unless it is absolutely necessary.

Responsibility is evident in the procedures you follow when working remotely because the virtual worker is held accountable in different ways than the traditional worker. While this is not necessarily a disadvantage, you may struggle with a new way of "keeping track" of the work you do. In a traditional office, "working" is often defined by the worker being physically present. The assumption is made that if you show up to work then you are working that day. This is far from the truth.

In the virtual office, "working" is defined by getting the job done. If the job does not get done, then the virtual worker did not "work" in the eyes of the boss. This brings about the need for more structure with clearly defined expectations. Technology tracks your positions and progress, when you are logged in, how long you were logged in, your email chat history and the web pages you visited. Some companies even install invisible programs on company-issued laptops so managers can spy on their remote employees. Managing the pajama worker is certainly a huge concern for employees as well as employers.

Before you shake your head in total abhorrence of these stealth technologies, you need to understand that the managerial challenges of the virtual workforce are exponential. These challenges are complex and related to distance, culture (internal and external), language and time, to name only a few. Cultural and functional differences may lead to a variety of different thought processes and obstacles. The freedom and mobility you experience can negatively impact productivity if you are left without support. All virtual workers need support and training on an ongoing basis as well as encouragement from leadership.

The virtual employee must feel trusted not only by his peers, but also by the boss. In his book, *The Speed of Trust*, Stephen R. Covey points out that trust equals confidence; therefore, when a supervisor trusts his employees, he is confident in their abilities and their integrity. In the virtual office, trust is at the heart of everything. Employees must be treated like the professionals they are and allowed to do the job they were hired to do. Mistrust has the tendency to rear its ugly head when management does not understand the needs of the virtual worker, or when the virtual worker does not understand the expectations of management. Trust issues in the virtual environment are imminent.

Noted management scholar Peter Drucker was one of the first to talk about management by results. In 1959, he coined the term "the knowledge worker" and indicated that management of knowledge workers was going to be one of the challenges for the 21st century. Although Drucker lived to see the beginning of the virtual workplace, he died at age 95 in 2005, the year Facebook was being launched (Drucker, 2006, 1964). It was Drucker who first brought us the concept that employees were valuable and should be considered assets of the company. Drucker said that what was important to the company was achieving results; management by observation was from an era that has long since disappeared. More credible than ever, his theory of management by results resonates in the virtual workplace.

Measuring productivity is more difficult when you can't do it by observation, so it presents another challenge in the virtual workplace. In the industrial age, productivity was highly tied to specialization. Performance was much more measurable when it was immediately observable, or so we pretended. In the virtual workplace, both performance and productivity must be evaluated differently. The degree to which a person is productive has to do with more than just what he/she does and where he/she does it. It is inexorably tied to the systems, procedures and people interacting with the virtual worker. In order for the virtual worker to function, the organization must define and communicate organizational goals, objectives, vision and mission. It must train virtual workers but also train managers to provide expectations, directives and evaluate the success of the project not only at the individual level but also at the team level.

Technology has made it possible for communication to become more multi-dimensional. Rather than only providing closeness or connectivity, you can manipulate digitally mediated communications to transmit or seek information. Today's social media revolution has also caused countless office quarrels and caused some individuals to lose their jobs because of something they posted on a social networking site. Take Michelle, for example, who faithfully updated her Facebook profile every morning. One day she commented on how stressful her job was and she was immediately terminated for negatively influencing co-workers. Then there is Octavia Nasr, who was fired from her position as Middle East editor for CNN after she tweeted about her political sentiments, which were considered to be anti-American. Remember: everything you say online can be used against you. Digital never forgets.

The idea of meaningfully connecting to others has really never changed. Today, however, we are inundated with so much information that the ability to meaningfully align communication with purpose is challenging. One common mistake is to blame technology for this dynamic shift, but it is the catalyst, not the cause.

Technology is a strong driving force behind change in human behavior. It provides different vehicles through which we communicate. You may choose to call from your smartphone, send an email or text. Each of these options is merely a different mode for delivering your message. It is humans that change their behavior when using technology, regardless of delivery mode. For example, think of the last time you went out to dinner with a friend or relative. And, instead of focusing on you, the other person became engrossed in a text exchange with someone else. Maybe it was the other way around, and you were the one paying more attention to your smartphone than to the human being physically next to you. Opportunities for communication abound but so do unintended consequences and the potential for chaos.

Humans by nature want to be effective contributors. The ways, means and methods of contribution in this digitally connected world are different. The rules are different. The playing field is different. We communicate differently and we interact differently. The patterns for sharing knowledge, learning and collaborating have also changed. Now you can record everything that is being said or done. There is a traceable record of everything in the virtual workplace. This alone certainly changes the way you learn, share and interact with others because you know you are being watched. While you may enjoy more personal privacy than the traditional worker because you can create your own work environment, as a virtual worker you actually have less professional privacy because the technology is constantly capturing your whereabouts. There is no turning back.

The world in which we live, work and play has changed. These changes are all-encompassing. They are omnipresent, universal and pervasive. In a 2007 report on unified communications, Frost and Sullivan Corporation characterized the growth of the virtual workplace as "one of the biggest business changes to hit in years." The human interactions that we have traditionally emphasized no longer suffice. The look in someone's eye may have to be determined online. We work, learn and play in a virtual world where we may never meet face to face with the folks we interact with. We work for companies we have never been to and we achieve degrees without setting foot in a classroom or on a campus. These new types of interactions have unforeseen consequences. This change in human interactions impacts individuals, organizations and society at large.

Today's virtual workplace is an environment full of stimuli. You are left to your own volition to turn off the cell phone, turn off the computer and disconnect from the demands of the virtual office. You are on your own to seek relaxation, joy and down time. The problem is, you do not know how to do this without feeling guilty. Only when you are able to act with autonomy, set and enact priorities, be authentically productive, make responsible choices, and align connections will you be able to get things under control and reap the benefits of the virtual workplace.

When Alexander Graham Bell shouted, "Mr. Watson – come here – I want to see you!" in 1876, he could not possibly have predicted that the basic idea behind the first telephone would morph into digital smartphones with so many capabilities. He probably never anticipated how his new gadget would forever change the way people communicate. The same idea lies behind current technologies. The technologies that connect us today will look completely different tomorrow. And they will inevitably impact the way you communicate when working, learning and socializing.

Even up to the present day, most people are still only talking about the technology itself and what you can do with it. The technology may be different, but the conversation is the same. *The Pajama Effect* forces you to reflect on your behaviors and ask yourself: "How have these behaviors changed because of how I use technology?" You live in this rapidly changing, digitally mediated world; consequently, there is no alternative but to care about what is happening around you. Even if you did your best to ignore it, you are immersed in it. Even if you are the last person on the planet to get connected, the fact is that your child, your spouse, your friend, your neighbor, your sibling or your co-worker is already connected, and the changes in his or her behavior will in turn have an impact on you.

No matter what you do for a living, your boss already expects that you have certain technology skills and that you can apply them in your day-to-day responsibilities. If your boss feels you would benefit from professional development, he or she may ask you to participate in an online training course or a hybrid course that has face-to-face components. The reality is that it is not cost-effective for companies to pay for your travels or for a day "off" for training purposes only. Many companies will now expect you to complete special training sessions online, but on your own time. When this happens, you cringe, bite your tongue, but eventually succumb to the pressures of the changing workplace. Let's face it: you want to keep your job. Without realizing it, you are blending your work life with your private life and learning through digitally mediated communications.

You should care about *The Pajama Effect* not only for your own sake, but also for the sake of the generation that follows. Whether it is your child, your niece, goddaughter or best friend's kid, younger people will face new challenges in the workplace of the future. You are positioned to be a pathfinder and role model for the next workforce. It is your responsibility to teach newer generations the skills they need to be successful in years to come. Although the challenges they will face will be different, the underlying struggle is the same: they will have to respond to changes around them as the boundaries and constraints of today's workplace have been removed.

The influence of technology on behavior is undeniable. You are part of an always-connected network of individuals, ideas, agendas and challenges. Your time is in high demand. Your boss may expect you to check your email on Sunday morning or your spouse may want you to answer text messages while you are writing a business proposal. You may have to stay home Saturday night and finish an assignment for an online class.

We react to these changes in many ways; sometimes successfully, but other times we stare into space, frustrated. We wish that someone could show us how to get everything done within the 24 hours a day we have been given.

The good news is that there is a way to work it out. It relates to not just where you work, but how you work. As you now already know, the virtual workplace has characteristics very different from most traditional office environments. The virtual office is characterized by openness, vulnerability, personal privacy, informality and detachment. As a result, you have increased flexibility, less external direction and you may experience a different kind of stress. There are things you can do to balance all your personal and professional responsibilities and diminish the stress you are under. This balance will let you be productive and successful.

Today, we have digital technologies; tomorrow, it may be something else. Holograms, artificial intelligence, virtual reality and faster, more integrated gadgets are sure to play a role in future forms of communication. These will cause us to modify and re-condition our current behaviors. This means that *The Pajama Effect* will continue to be a part of the way we blend our private and professional lives for a long time to come. We will always have to find new ways of coping with the unavoidable changes. The environments that we consider normal now will soon be outdated and replaced. Once again we will be out of our element and dealing with a new environment where the boundaries and constraints no longer apply.

As stated earlier, technologies have been a driving force in establishing *The Pajama Effect*. This new behavioral and physiological phenomenon affects the individual, the organization and society. It is highly unlikely that the changes that have already taken place will ever be reversed. You must be in a position to survive the sea of change but also to emerge as a valued professional and balanced individual. To be successful in the digital environment, you need to manage the skills you have while learning new skill sets, new perspectives and improving your ability to respond to the pressures around you.

When you hear yourself saying things like, "I am trying to make the best of the situation," ask yourself if this is becoming an excuse. Trying your best means giving yourself the opportunity to learn the skills you need to be successful and get the tools necessary to make it happen. Or, as Star Wars character Yoda famously said, "Do. Or do not. There is no try." The privacy you have in the comfort of your virtual office may cause you to do things you would not do in the traditional office space.

The digital world is one of dichotomy: on one hand, there is a sense of privacy, but on the other hand everything is being recorded by the communications. Be aware of the traps you set for yourself, the excuses and the negative self-talk: "I tried doing it and it didn't work out, so it's okay." Light your own path and arm yourself with the courage to say, "I will succeed," and believe it.

Virtual Touch Points

Leading, Inspiring, & Measuring Performance in the Virutal Workplace

Exerpt

Technology is not technology if it happened before you were born.
—Sir Ken Robinson

Managing the Invisible

There has been a significant shift in the workplace in the last decade toward "intellectual capital" and a reframing of the role of manager as one of leader. Gone are the days of being able to tell if a worker is a good one because he or she spends exorbitant amounts of time behind the desk. The age of the knowledge worker ushered in a time of "knowing," an era when what was important was in your mind not on the assembly line. Good soldiers, you see, were broken. Their independence sacrificed for the cause. Their intellectual spark vanished because they lost something important in the battle of control. They lost their ability to think and act with autonomy. They lost the ability to think for themselves.

In many organizations, leadership is lost. They have little or no idea how to inspire and measure performance in the virtual world. They are lost in a paradigm of the past, one that says management should influence and control. In the virtual world, in contrast, it is essential for the individual to be authentically productive. The real reason people get called back to the office is not one of collaboration and inspiration but one of trust. When workers are not in a face to face environment, leadership is not sure how to tap into the creativity, innovation and productivity of their workforce. It is not the economy, business cycle, outsourcing or offshoring that is the problem. It is lack of individual support and empowerment. Manage comes from a root word that is the same as the one used for "manipulate" or "maneuver," and means to change something to fit a purpose. The image of the good soldier willing to sacrifice everything for the cause is still alive in some organizations. However, even in corporate cultures long known for this, the mentality is beginning to change. Power is the ability to act with autonomy. To create and innovate you need the freedom to act without judgment.

Innovation in many organizations has become as extinct as Tyrannosaurus rex. This is really a dilemma in a world of constant change. Success seems to depend on adapting to the new. Some organizations are waking up to the need to empower people. This requires inspiring them to think for themselves so that they can respond creatively to the relentless change that surrounds them. Other are still operating in a fear-based mentality. They are afraid of what they cannot see. They are afraid of losing control and afraid of the soldiers deserting. The Harvard Business Review writes books about innovation and the Economist runs articles on creativity. But what really needs to happen will not be created by essay. It will be inspired by technology and the freedom inherent in the virtual environment.

Technology gives us the ability to be independent yet connected. You can be at basketball practice in a high school gym in Philadelphia and have a meeting with someone in Japan. If you have a cellphone, tablet or a laptop and a connection you can engage in global commerce. Access to world markets is easy. Organizations are starting to understand that managing people that work in this detached but connected environment might require a new approach.

Businesses and organizations are using **Created by** technology exponentially to communicate and **Technology** organize "Big Data." The hope is that the organization can impact the bottom line either by lowering costs or driving revenue. Technology provides opportunities to respond to global markets and create new relationships that may be advantageous. Technology allows people to interact, engage and share experiences without being physically together. This ability to interact without physical presence is what happens in the virtual environment. These new environments exist because they can.

Changes fueled by an unlimited technology arsenal impact our relationships at work. Consultants, micro workers and experts are available to organizations. A global workforce at your fingertips provides both speed and reach. Compensation practices, the layout of the workplace and job expectations are under scrutiny. Organizations are rethinking what "good looks like." They are attempting to break down silos (isolation), embrace and not limit vacations, have casual days every day and share visions. This technology is also disruptive and has the impact of changing not only where we work but how.

The virtual workplace is here. People rely on electronic communication and virtual connectivity to get their jobs done. This reliance on technology has created an environment that has a double edge. You are both isolated and constantly connected. More than 50 million people travel less but work just as effectively using technology. They don't have to be in the office and they don't need to travel for meetings either. To some extent this technology has been liberating. People don't have to do long commutes, sit in traffic or fight the weather. They can work at home in their "pajamas" if they choose. The new environment is a more relaxed, less structured and more flexible environment than the traditional workplace. Remote access with web-based technology, collaboration tools and smart devices supports flexible work environments and adaptive schedules. It also appears to be flatter.

You can have a direct connection to higher levels of management. These people, who were unapproachable in the face to face (F2F) world, are a Tweet or an email away. But there is another much darker and disturbing side to the virtual environment. It is an environment of paradoxes, of opposites and of contradictions. Authority, authenticity, privacy, accountability and identity are only a few of the dichotomies facing the virtual workplace. The old structures are falling but slowly. Like the coliseum in Rome, position, rewards and recognition from another time are still standing in many organizations.

Not All That Flat   Personal devices give us the impression of one to one communication. Research as far back as the 1960s on human to computer interactions reinforces the fact that we like to relate to devices in a one to one, personal way. We relate to the device as if we were talking to another human being, which sometimes we are and sometimes we are not. It is an illusion that since we adopted social networks everyone one is on the same level and everyone is accessible. After all, we can receive personal "Tweets" from rock stars, presidential candidates and football heroes. Authority, however, is still an issue in most organizations. The hierarchy, the chain of command, salary structures and corporate ladders are remnants from a different time and are just starting to be phased out. Collaboration is now disrupted by an old paradigm of authority and power. Speed and access are a part of this. The ability to collaborate or reach and create relationships with other people is also an influence on organizational change. Value in the virtual workplace is created through connections with others.

Power formerly came from hierarchy, position and compensation. The virtual workplace reduces barriers to entry and achievement. Organizational rituals like F2F meetings and sitting in the "power positions" at the heads of the table or right across from the boss are archaic and outdated in the virtual environment. The traditional ways of relating through control, influence and intimidation just don't work here. The job descriptions of the past also don't work, and that makes organizations very nervous. In the virtual environment, there are no corner offices, executive restrooms or preferred parking spaces. Many leadership, innovation and change management theories are obsolete in this new era. These models are derived from paradigms of the past. Without the benefits of charisma and immediate authority, it becomes less about structure and progression and more about availability and opportunity.

Working relationships tend to take on a new meaning when there are no traditional delineators of power. Authentic productivity and contributions are what count. The traditional chain of command and authority is being challenged. Working in the virtual world tests more than giving up collaboration at the water cooler. It challenges organizations to replace power based on charisma and authority with power based on expertise and contribution. We are changing not only how we manage but what we manage. We used to manage people, now we manage results.

Virtual work environments shine a light on the competing values of yesterday and today. Many organizations are reluctant to change. They are content with power networks and visibility that can demand recognition and reward. Traditional notions of executive power and hierarchy are part of Western culture. Most of what is written and researched about virtual teams is based on antiquated team theory from the last century. This is revisited and updated in a flawed attempt to reflect the virtual environment.

It is a challenge for human beings to integrate the new without reference to the context of the old. The virtual environment with all its side shows, big data, constant connectivity, global reach and boundless everything creates a very different challenge for leadership. Virtual teams are flatter and they cut across silos and infrastructures. For the last thirty years, organizations have looked to teams to increase performance. Virtual teams are more flexible, creative and fluent. They get a great deal of work done. Technology enables the transition to a virtual work environment, and virtual teams are playing a much larger role in the economics of business.

Having a virtual workforce, however, also creates many business benefits for the organization that cannot be ignored. The virtual worker gets freedom and flexibility not only over where they live but how and the organization gets to hire valuable talent wherever that talent resides. The ability to hire regardless of location, an expanded talent pool, lower real estate costs, a reduction in business and travel expenses and happier and more productive workers are only a few of the benefits. Workers have a more flexible lifestyle and spend more time with their families. It saves everybody money and provides opportunities for people who may otherwise not be able to be a part of the workforce. The virtual workplace creates value to the environment as well. It cuts down on gasoline consumption and decreases smog and pollution. But the true value comes from what the virtual worker can contribute both in terms of knowledge and performance.

When power and performance are not part of the same structure this can create problems within the organization. A significant amount of research has been conducted in the last decade, and most of it suggests that organizations are reluctant to give up the hierarchy. Virtual teams are good at circumventing structure to facilitate speed and availability. Organizational structure can vanish while accomplishing project objectives and goals but the hierarchy remains. The hierarchy operates outside of the world of the virtual environment. In many cases it is still alive and well in the C Suite at corporate headquarters.

Very little research exists on what happens to power when the organization is horizontal. What has happened to this point is that organizations have relied on the past. We have tried to apply theories of management and leadership that are centuries old to the virtual environment (Hornett, 2004).

Organizations do not want to give up the power structure. This makes it very difficult to manage the invisible. There is a lot more invisible in the lack of support for virtual workers than the fact they are just working off site.

Virtual workers struggle with invisibility. They are concerned that what they do is not seen or recognized by the organization's leadership. Does management know how hard I'm working? How do I know what is really going on because no one tells me anything? They often feel like they are out of sight, out of mind and out of touch. Virtual workers also struggle with finding their "off" button. A common complaint is "I feel like I am always on. I am always working." They lack boundaries, both personal and professional, and often feel like they are being exploited. But more importantly they don't feel like they are part of the club. Organizations are currently not very likely to support virtual workers in a way that strengthens them as individuals or as productive performers within the organization.

Value is created in the virtual workplace by offering both flexibility and strong support. Employees need to be given the freedom and the power to run their own show, to create the balance between their work commitments and their personal lives. Management needs to communicate clearly the business objectives that must be met and provide the road map to get there. Expectations need to be more clearly defined, check-ins more frequent, and collaboration more regular. This lowers risk of stress on the individual. It allows fear to dissolve and creativity and innovation to flourish.

True value is developed through encouraging and supporting innovation and creativity. Creativity and innovation are only fostered when the mission is transparent and the communication and expectations are clear. Creativity has a much better chance of thriving in a diverse and global environment. The organization wants to support this talent by developing the skills that give virtual workers the resources to explore a global range of challenges and perspectives.

Working virtually means both the worker and the organization need to develop a different set of core skills. Working in the virtual environment means greater freedom, and with greater freedom comes more responsibility. The ability to act with autonomy and self-manage is only one part of the skill set. Workers also need to be able to set and enact priorities, be authentically productive, make responsible choices and align connections (Baggio, 2014). Virtual workers need the confidence and self-reliance to overcome obstacles, the self-discipline and personal project management skills to get work done on time and contribute their expertise. But the organization needs to get involved in this process also.

Organizations need to encourage this type of behavior, to allow the employee to take ownership of their work, their schedule and their performance. They need to empower the employee and encourage them to succeed. They need to support engagement and productivity through clearly communicated expectations, well defined performance goals and mutually agreed upon objectives. And then, most importantly, they need to let the employee go. The biggest challenge to success in the virtual environment is leadership. Leading virtually means leading differently. Leaders in the virtual workplace should listen between the lines and communicate clearly and intuitively. They need to have and to communicate clear expectations for performance, accountability and measurement.

Goals, deadlines and accountabilities create the roadmap for success. These need to be defined, communicated and reinforced. Leadership will also want to be transparent. Deceitful practices and hidden agendas do not do well in the virtual environment. This is an environment where trust is paramount and lack of trust can sabotage even the best of intentions. Trust is difficult to gain and easy to lose. No virtual workplace can succeed without trust in strong leaders.

Leaders in the virtual workplace need enhanced capabilities to manage independent and autonomous individuals. The old methods do not work. They need advanced communication skills, intuitive listening skills, trust building, and inspirational skills, and above all strong project management and accountability. They need to be able to deal with ambiguity and change and to reach and connect in a way that supports both the virtual worker and the business's objectives. The virtual leader needs to be focused on and deliver results. Value in the virtual workplace is all about delivering the goods. This ability comes by aligning connections. It is the job of virtual leadership to set up enough touchpoints and the right touchpoints to get this done.

The virtual world is all about connections and connecting. Leaders in the virtual environment need to be effective communicators. They need to build relationships in an environment that is fast paced, remote and where distractions abound. To build a relationship, you have to touch someone. Not necessarily physically but certainly emotionally and cognitively. Relationships are built on touchpoints. Touchpoint is a term used to describe the interface between two things. Companies interface with customers and employees though many different channels: distribution, communication, service, public relations, investor relations and human resources. Virtual leadership is about creating and supporting touchpoints. Touchpoint leadership is a multi-dimensional strategic approach that focuses on optimizing performance.

Touchpoints

Touchpoint leadership creates relationships that support the whole person and meet the business's objectives. This is customarily done through roles. In relationships, people play roles. This is how they connect. For example, in a marriage someone is a "husband" and someone is a "wife." In a friendship, both parties are "friends." In relationships, these roles often come with preconceived meaning. Developing meaning that works for both sides is one of the big challenges to leading in the virtual world. One of the biggest obstacles of leading a virtual workforce successfully is a traditional management mindset. Notice that roles are nouns. In the virtual work environment, we are interested in verbs. Performance and results are achieved with verbs.

Creating touchpoints in the virtual work environment is not always easy or automatic. The economics of virtual work, however, makes it an undertaking that can bring very positive bottom line results for the business and the individual. The first step is to get honest, and take stock of where you are and where you want to be. Leaders are often in denial about fear, loss of control, the "I can't see them I can't manage them" mentality. What more commonly surfaces is a distorted rational that claims "We need to be together to bond, collaborate, and create," which is just an excuse for "I don't trust them. If I am not watching them, they are not working, and I don't know how to control that or motivate these people!"

Touchpoints come in many different sizes and shapes. There are three general categories or types of touchpoints required to lead, inspire and measure virtual workplace performance: conceptual, transactional, and actual. Each of these general categories can be broken down into other categories. What is important is not the labels. What is critical is that the organization realizes that it touches the virtual worker in many ways, some invisible, some prescribed and some real.

Conceptual touchpoints include the organizational culture, shared perceptions, and views. Conceptual touchpoints can include many different channels from branding to social media to any number of internal and external influences. Conceptual touchpoints include the semantics of the organization and the intangible influences that can affect human behaviors. This includes how the organization knows itself, expresses itself and identifies the fundamental things that make it what it is. It can include the little things some individuals deal with day to day. There are internal and external conceptual touchpoints. Conceptual touchpoints are invisible and intangible but still influence the performance of the individual. Often, we attribute these to the organizational culture and the economic climate.

Transactional touchpoints are operational interfaces that impact how work gets done. These are the organizational charts, procedure manuals, business processes, operational diagrams, performance requirements or anything else that seeks to capture relationships of importance within the organization. This can be the basis for the actual touchpoints but the two should not be confused. Often, they are not the same. Transactional touchpoints include the organization's business strategy, the political structures and the information systems. Transactional touchpoints include procedures and frameworks. Companies develop these in many ways. Frequently they are distinct to the organization, people, and market. These touchpoints are often entrenched in history and seldom examined.

Actual touchpoints are the interfaces that really happen. These are the interactions between leaders and workers, workers and workers, worker and the organizational infrastructure, and workers and their performance tasks. These are the real interactions. Vicarious touchpoints are actual touchpoints that are observed from a distance. Actual touchpoints are the procedures and processes we really experience, both the good and not so good.

Touchpoints affect the emotional, mental and physical wellbeing of the virtual worker. They can be very supportive and provide reassurance or very disruptive and contribute to stress and anxiety. There can be too many or not enough touchpoints. They can be restrictive or supportive and imagined or real. The challenge is to establish touchpoints that both support the virtual worker and meet the business objects. Although flexibility, responsiveness and connections are important, what really matters in the virtual workplace is results (Rea & Field, 2012).

Listening Between the Lines

Organizations and other individuals touch us in many ways. Organizations are essentially networks of people who are joined together through interactions and form relationships. Communicating expectations, goals, objectives, deadlines, knowledge, support and efficacy cements relationships. A wide range of work environments may be considered to be virtual: global work teams, geographically dispersed project teams, inter-organizational groups, non-traditional work places (hotels, home or work centers) and non-traditional roles (micro workers, experts or consultants). Team structures and communication procedures unite or separate people in the virtual environment. Effective leaders not only know how to navigate within the structures and procedures, they know how to read between the lines (Watson-Manheim & Belanger, 2002).

At the heart of performance is communication-based work practices. These practices can be accomplished by conversations. In the virtual world, how those practices take place depends not only on the individuals involved but on the technology used and the affordances of that technology. The virtual environment is complex and the modes for communication areas exploding. In the virtual environment multiplicity is the norm. It is normal for virtual worker to use a multitude of different technologies and work at a variety of locations.

It is also typical to work with a wide variety of colleagues from many different areas. The virtual worker usually works on an assortment of teams and assumes many different roles simultaneously. They may belong to several task forces, work on several project teams, and belong to a department or division or a work group. What develops is multiple relationships. Managing multiple relationships can be challenging. If we can eliminate the obvious, and assume that communicating via all these different technologies is not the same as being in a F2F meeting, then the question becomes: What do we need to do to use these technologies effectively and support virtual workers and the organization?

Relationships and emotional connections in a world geographically distributed are extremely important. Many organizations have a huge challenge with onboarding for this reason. It is important to know who to call when you need something and then how to read the person when they respond. Many people find it difficult to be effective until they know the right people and establish the right relationships. Relationship development is clearly a pathway to success. Collecting information and sharing knowledge effects performance success. (Watson-Manheim & Belanger, 2002).

Many managers and supervisors in the virtual environment need to learn new communication skills and intuitive listening. The level and effectiveness of this type of listening impacts information overload and establishes trust and reliance. Creating personal relationships and developing trust when there are limited facial expressions, physical cues and body language requires creating new and different touchpoints. This usually means more communication and touching base more frequently. Regular updates and status reports will help, but intuitive listening is about more than formal communication channels. It is the ability to read people eyes, their faces, their expressions on video chats and their tone of voice in emails. This allows us to touch the other person at just the right time and in just the right way. Communicating in the virtual environment requires unconventional thinking and a willingness to take a few calculated risks (Rea & Field, 2012).

What we say and what we mean are not always the same. Human beings are complex social animals. They have an inherent desire to know what their territory looks like and how to find their place in it. Often this is done with messages that fly below the radar. Reading these messages takes discipline and a well–tuned willingness to connect with the individual. This is a very different mindset than an approach that struggles to maintain control over people, projects, and deadlines. Many managers believe that virtual collaboration can undermine authority. Trust or lack of trust is what happens when we fear we are losing control when we can't see what is going on. One of the biggest challenges in leading in the virtual workplace is the change in mindset. Managers are no longer managing people's time and activities. They are accountable for results. Being responsible for results require leaders to step up and take ownership.

Silver, Halpern and Roselle, LLC is a national accounting firm whose main business is in three areas: Accounting, Tax and Audit. Their reputation is excellent and is based on great service and trust. Their customers respect them, trust their advice and stay with them for a long time. This reputation is achieved by state of the art computer systems, analytical databases and a variety of tools the managers and accountants use when consulting with the clients. Most of these programs are custom to Silver, Halpern and Roselle.

The firm hires expert technical people to develop and maintain the custom applications that support the business. The software applications integrate tax laws and the coding is extremely technical. It requires attention to detail and a high level of skill. The people who write these custom computer applications must be proficient in both tax law and programming skills. New tax laws are always being applied for the United States and foreign countries. These changes must be integrated into the existing systems quickly and flawlessly or the fallout could be very detrimental.

There are four programmers that work as subcontractors for Silver, Halpern and Roselle. They live in New York, Boston and Philadelphia. Everyone is on the East Coast of the United States. They only get together twice a year at the Silver, Halpern and Roselle holiday party and at the summer company picnic. They are connected to each other via email, a synchronous/video-chat platform and telephone. Formal meetings are rare but it is not at all unusual for informal meetings to occur among the programing staff.

Meet the Staff   George Anderson is a tax lawyer, a graduate of University of Massachusetts and a former hockey player. He is married with three young children and has a wife who works full time in downtown Boston. He is the stay-at-home Dad and 35 years old. George has been working for Silver, Halpern and Roselle for eight years and is the oldest and longest standing member of the programming group. He is responsible for all system analytics and design changes. George also functions as the trainer and onboarding specialist. He is the main contact point for the group and is the "team leader" and ultimately responsible for projects being on time and meeting the budget. He is also busy with soccer games, coaching baseball, dance lessons and basic household duties. He lives in a suburban area of Boston.

Carol Creig is a tax accountant and computer science double major from Boston College. She is 32 years old and has been with the group for two years. She is single and lives on a farm in New Hampshire and loves hunting and fishing. Carol is a full time partner and rarely comes into the city.

Margaret Harrison is a tax lawyer and a Wharton MBA. She lives in the Chestnut Hill area of Philadelphia and is 39 years old. Currently single, she likes to golf and play tennis and travel. She has been with the team four years and enjoys her autonomy. She works out of her apartment.

Jim Morrelli is a programmer and lives in New York. His wife is a corporate attorney and they have four children ages twelve, six, four and two. They have an apartment in the city and all the children go to public schools. Jim is interested in his job but he is also a base guitarist and plays in a band.

The main way this team communicates is via email. They send many emails back and forth every day. They can call or text each other anytime. They meet on Monday morning by video chat and have a rule that when you are online you have the chat stream open. They are all hourly employees except for George who was made a salaried employee last year. They have an agreement that they can work wherever and whenever they way want as long as the work gets done on time. Flexibility is important to all of them and their lifestyles. They enjoy their freedom and none of them plans on ever working in an office full time again.

Jim is a classic programmer and loves to create code that helps him to update these systems more quickly. On a recent project, he created a "shortcut" that allowed them to get the job done in much less time than it usually takes. The problem came in when they realized that this was cutting into Carol, Margaret and especially Jim's wages, because all three are paid by the hour. Rather than tell George about the shortcut, they kept it from him because they feared he would tell his boss and then they would make less money. They could have more personal time if they met the deadlines and used the shortcut. This all worked well for a while.

In a casual conversation Margaret was having with a friend over lunch who knows several people who work at the firm, she leaked that they had an innovation that was giving them a great deal of time and that they now had more free time for their own interests. Margaret talked to her friend and her friend talked to Art Silver. Art is George's boss. Art became very concerned because no one had mentioned this to him. He wondered what the shortcut was and why the billable hours had not changed. He contacted George. George assured him that he knew nothing about this, but rather than this making Art feel better, he became more concerned. If George didn't know this was going on, what else didn't he know? Art decided to call everyone back into the office, Jim and Margaret informed the company that they were not about to move.

AI and the Agile Workplace

How Artificial Intelligence is Changing the Way We Work

Exerpt

The promise of artificial intelligence and computer science generally vastly outweighs the impact it could have on some jobs in the same way that, while the invention of the airplane negatively affected the railroad industry, it opened a much wider door to human progress.

—Paul Allen

Chapter 1

The Robots Aren't Coming, They're Here

AI has become an everyday thing. The major ecosystems in AI are popping up everywhere in our lives. Google is saying "Happy Birthday" and Amazon's Alexa is asking if there is anything else, she can do after she has turned off the lights. We pull into the drive-in window at McDonald's or walk into a Panera and the conversation is with "bots" (voice recognition technologies), not people. It's hard these days to talk with a human: at work, online and even at the train station. Bots have taken over. Barriers to entry, that kept AI at bay for decades, somehow have slipped away, and a wide range of products, services and applications have emerged. right under our noses. Society hasn't really felt the disruption yet. Not like we will in the next decade. Estimates of worker displacement range between 48% in the US to 70% in India. Humans just were not paying attention. AI is no longer a future technology. It is here now. It is here to stay.

Finally, the focus is starting to shift toward impact. Terms like big data, little data, machine learning, deep learning are part of our vocabulary. Scientists aren't just thinking about how this works, but how can this work for people, now. AI and robots using this kind of intelligence are everywhere. From Marty the robot at the local grocery store who roams the isles asking if he can help locate products, to the voices that pop up on the smart phone, AI

225

has been deployed. The engineering part is being conquered. Now it is a question of shared vision. What do we want AI to do? How can it help people? How will it reframe business processes? Everyone, not just technical people, need to play a role in these decisions. AI is here and ready to solve problems for everyone in all aspects of their lives.

AI took a long time coming but now that it is here, it demands respect. Researchers, engineers, designers, dialogue experts, voice talent, inclusion and diversity experts and many more talented people need to be involved. Otherwise humanity is in big trouble. The results could be not only troubling but very inhumane. AI is moving quickly, very quickly. It has taken on a life of its own. Anyone who is responsible for redundant and repetitive tasks is at risk of being replaced. AI is about making decision and judgements, things that in the past were part of only the human domain. It is ripe with complexities, challenges, and potential. AI is taking on problems, discovering unrealized opportunities, and identifying new actions. It can and will solve problems. It will find its way into almost every nook and cranny of every industry and every aspect of our lives.

AI has been on the horizon for decades. AI has been coming for a long while. Since the mid 1940's when conversations on understanding the nature of intelligent thought laid the foundations for information processing, challenges and fantasy have been mixed with influence and ideas from many disciplines. It has always held the promise of imagined possibilities, infinite promise and defining what it means to be human. Philosophers from Gottfried Wilhelm Leibniz to Blaise Pascal, very early on reflected on the design of intelligent machines. Jules Verne, Isaac Asimov, Frank Baum (who wrote the Wizard of Oz) and many others imagined responsive devices capable of communication with human beings and supporting and challenging our deepest concerns on being human. (Buchanan, 2006).

Both the fields of AI and Machine Learning (ML) have grown well beyond any of the individual contributors. Nobert Wiener's work on cybernetics, W. Ross Ashby, Warren McCulloch and Walter Pitt's work on neural networks, contributions from communication theory, mathematics and statistics, logic and philosophy, linguistics and of course John Von Neumann and Oskar Morgenstern, in game theory have left their mark on AI and ML. The landmark paper in Mind, 1950 which led to the landmark imitation game, known as Turing's Test, was a major turning point in this evolutionary journey. The name AI was given at the 1956 Dartmouth conference on Artificial Intelligence. As this discussion unfolds over the decades, when AI is described, at the core of intelligence is always the concept of continued learning.

Most of AI today, like it was in the 1960's, is based on semantic information processing. Language, understanding and translation were always thought to be the cornerstone of AI because of the computer's ability to store and retrieve huge amounts of verbal data, phrases and massive dictionaries. Gradually, understanding began to creep into the landscape and language understanding and translations have moved AI closer to providing humans with non-human conversant assistants. Knowledge based systems have overtaken logic-based paradigms.

Slowly since the 1960's MIT, IBM, CMU, Stanford and many other think tanks have helped move AI forward. Today AAAI, the Association for the Advancement of Artificial Intelligence, is a thriving association serving the AI community.

AI and intelligent human behavior is not easily defined. Generally, AI describes the process of machines doing work that would require human intelligence. The term generally includes investigating intelligence, problems solving and creating computers systems that are intelligent. Sometimes AI is described as weak or strong. Weak AI implies a computer is merely mimicking cognitive processes and simulating intelligence. Strong AI implies computers are self-learning and intelligent. Computers can understand and optimize their own behaviors based on prior knowledge or data and experiences (Wisskirchen, 2017). Other ways of describing AI include narrow, broad and channel. Narrow AI is the ability of AI to handle one specific task for the purpose of duplicating or replacing human intelligence. Diagnosing in radiology or skin cancer is often used as an example of narrow AI. Broad AI is systems that are capable of exhibiting intelligent behaviors across many processes or tasks. Broad AI systems may even exhibit other aspects of human intelligence someday. Channel AI is even broader, more influencing and more expansive (Growth Stage Podcast, 2018).

AI from its beginning has been plagued with duality. Success in AI has always been accompanied by increased responsibility, social responsibilities, educational challenges and impact that decision makers and the general public vaguely understand. Considerable progress has been made in understanding the how and what of AI, including common modes of reasoning. Research shows, that combinations of deductive, case based, inductive, uncertainty, and default reasoning are just a few of the aspects of intelligence that are necessary for successful AI systems. The duality between the role of humans in the universe and what role machines will play, is only beginning to play out. AI offers humans benefits, including less boring repetitive workplaces, safer manufacturing, better travel, increased security, and smarter decisions that may help preserve a volatile habitat (Buchanan, 2006).

Since the beginning, AI has been concerned with creating intelligent machines that formalize reasoning and understanding in all areas of the human experience. The direction has always been toward formalizing knowledge in a way that makes working with computers easier and more helpful. The impact of AI on living has the potential to meet and or exceed the impact of any prior technologies. Exploring psychology, reasoning, decision science and behavior puts AI in the position to solve intellectual problems, control robot motions, interpret human language, learn new skills and acquire knowledge by continually analyzing data.

What is so disconcerting about the robots being here, is that they have been coming for so long and suddenly, they are everywhere. AI has become an everyday technology. It is the start of a new chapter in human history. A chapter that can and will have greater impact than almost anyone can imagine. A wide range of services, products and sources have contributed to the emergence of AI as an everyday technology. It is time for our focus to shift from the technical aspects of AI to the impact it will have on human lives. It is no longer about will it happen or how the technology can work, but rather what can it do for us and how will we be impacted both positively and negatively by this revolution. We have entered the world of everyday AI.

With every technology comes displacement and upheaval. The workforce is transformed and rearranged. AI is certainly no exception and has the potential to be the most disruptive yet. Business will drive the deployment of AI. Human's in every aspect of society, need to be involved in the voice that contributes to how AI is used.

AI is both accessible and powerful. It has the potential to do a tremendous amount of good. It also has the potential to turn our world upside down, displacing millions in the workplace, eliminating jobs and creating voids as well as opportunities. AI is ready to solve problems and take over redundant and menial tasks. Are humans ready to adapt and relearn? To create a new kind of workplace? One that is not based on the old vision of transactions, widgets and repetition? One that works towards fulfilling the needs of the people, not just business? AI meets people where they are. Whether it is a chatbot on a website or an app, or a robot on the assembly line, AI goes to the need.

AI requires monitoring because it is moving so quickly. Robots are displacing people in almost all areas, it is just a question of who and how. This means looking clearly at the technology. High quality, reliable, consistent data is a must with a continued awareness on the impact on the human experience. Humans are ultimately responsible for the decisions AI is making. Automating cognition, judgment and reason is not without challenges. AI has a role to play in almost every industry which means it is mainstream and can and will have a huge impact on our workplace. It's time to talk. It's time to get a plan. Humanity is moving forward, and very quickly with deployed AI (Moore, 2019).

From HR, to the production floor there is a great emphasis on using AI to support rapid change and create a better human experience. The disruption is rampant. Industries, sectors, products and positions are being transformed before our eyes. Uber disrupted the transportation business, AirBnB the hotel business and Amazon just about every business. The question becomes one of speed and adaption. This requires a fundamental shift in how people view work. Work is no longer about just hiring people and tracking hours worked. It is about productivity, and the ability to respond quickly to changes in market conditions, customer demands and technological innovations. What will be done by the robots and what will require human intervention? Business will need to hire smarter and train better. It will be imperative for businesses to hire and keep the best talent. The world of robots makes treating humans with respect imperative. Human seek more from work than robots. They need connection, meaning, value, development and acknowledgement.

The workplace and the educational system have to keep up with the rest of the world. Advances in technologies have made the world more accessible, convenient and enjoyable. AI, chatbots, vocally activated technology, machine learning, social platforms, mobile apps and a host of other technologies, like virtual reality, mixed reality, adaptive technologies have found their way into our workplaces (Oracle, 2019).

AI also offers tremendous potential for production, monitoring machines, performing quality control checks, and regulating power. It can make production more efficient, reliable and less dependent on humans. Flexibility is the biproduct of AI on the production floor. Data is everywhere and being analyzed constantly. This is bringing prices down and quality up. Using data in real time to adjust and create a flexible manufacturing process has enormous potential. Using AI for customizing products and small production runs revolutionizes manufacturing. From production robots to automated virtual assistants, Price Waterhouse Cooper (PwC) suggests nearly 62% of large companies are currently using AI. Quality control, testing and machine maintenance are only a few applications. Many solutions are going to the cloud where data can be gathered internationally on the manufacturing process linking products, plants, processes, machines and systems. It is all about optimizing production and making smart decisions just in time. Production becomes more reliable, products more dependable and companies more efficient.

All of this has happened very quickly. Although we have been foreseeing and experimenting with AI for decades, the deployment of AI reached a tipping point only recently. This puts a tremendous strain on the IT infrastructure of any organization and raises big.... Or rather huge questions about risk, security and safeguards. Cybercrime is becoming more sophisticated and prevalent. Comprehensive security surrounding plants, facilities and even cities has everyone scrambling for new measures and better implementation. AI and increased threat through digitization go hand in hand.

Machine learning, deep learning, natural language processing and computer vision are being invested in by companies determined to reap the benefits of deployed AI. The level of support for the adoption of AI is basic economics. Better, faster, cheaper is the promise but it will take talent and planning to make it happen. The more AI, especially cloud-based applications, the less it costs to get in the game. It is a balancing act between creating new cognitive technologies and effective execution of those technologies so that they benefit everyone. There is no shortage of enthusiasm or investment, but effective execution might be another story.

Systems with huge cloud-based data sets like CRM (Customer Relationship Management) and ERP (Enterprise Resource Planning) systems are open doors for deploying AI across the enterprise. CRM is software that lets the company to track every transaction with the clients and customers. ERP refers to software program that helps the business to manage its processes, going on across the enterprise. Companies are finding it easier and easier as more and more vendors get on the bandwagon. Modifying and customizing off the shelf applications is replacing build from scratch applications like HR recruitment, payroll and retention. The cost and initial risk is coming down. More companies are turning to vendors for cloud-based solutions. Everyone is getting in the game. It is all about competition. Adaptation of AI is seen as a competitive advantage and of critical strategic importance. Finally, the expectations for transformation are slowing a bit. This is because we are recognizing the complexities of deployed AI. From the impact on the infrastructure, to training and education, how we use AI and how we protect ourselves while using AI is a balancing act and one that society has not quite mastered. The promise of better, faster cheaper or enhanced products and processes and better decision making is off set by the realities and dangers of digitization.

Healthcare is probably the most visible in terms of industries with high potential but so far, lower impact. Radiology and claims management have been a success and again show that redundant process, cognitive or task oriented will be replaced. Once people get involved the deployment of AI successfully, can be more challenging. Humans always complicate things. There is undoubtably huge potential that will continue to unfold in this area, that will help humans and make the healthcare industry more efficient and cost effective.

When business processes change, every aspect needs to be examined. There are very few cases where robots are totally replacing the humans. More likely, AI is augmenting the business process and hopefully making it more efficient, effective and flexible. In most cases humans are not being eliminated but rather supported. Any kind of change though takes education and support. Change is not easy and not something that humans naturally embrace.

The reality is that effectively deploying AI requires companies and organizations to become experts in exactly what most of them are not good at; risk management, flexibility and change. In other words, agile. Many companies have seen AI projects fail not because the technologies are inferior but because the humans who use the technologies are not ready to accept and act on the recommendations. When humans neither understand nor trust technologies the results can be less than optimal.

AI also shines a spotlight on areas of neglect within a company; the structure of internal systems that lack interconnectivity and have a considerable amount of redundancy. AI is all about the data and the data must have integrity. Customer data is in one system, financial data in another, HR data in another and on and on... these systems have never been integrated. AI requires data early and lots of it. Many companies just find it too difficult and costly to mine the data from multiple systems while protecting privacy, security and having data integrity.

There is no question that deployed AI has a set of risk factors all its own. Deep learning, a term used to describe machine learning involving neural networks, is used in image and speech recognition but is really not understood by most humans. Fear of disruption, threats of infiltration and security risk are clouding the safety and reliability of AI systems. System failure and how much data and what kind add to the complexity of implementation. Life on the cloud for data has gained in popularity in recent years but many companies and organizations are still very concerned about risks vs. benefits.

The arrival of AI on a much larger scale has also opened questions of privacy. Although the robots are here, very little has been put into place as far as legal and regulatory preparations. Europe currently has the General Data Protection Regulation (GDPR) but the US, China, India and other countries are lagging. There is no question that cloud-based data has changed the way we connect the world. Explaining how computer models behave can be a complex and difficult endeavor even if the willingness to do so exists. Regulators are challenged with deep learning and tend to look at these AI models like black holes. The results can be very accurate but how they were derived remains a mystery. Many companies involved in AI feel the necessity to explain "how we got there" and are pouring huge amounts of money into explain-ability. Whether it is the Facebook debacle or the issue of fake news in the 2016 US elections, nearly everyone realizes there is an issue with false information and AI. Misuse of personal data can affect important life decisions like credit worthiness, crime detection, and bias. Bias data can generate discriminatory results. So, the arrival of AI is not without challenges. One study showed that Google showed ads for high paying jobs more to men than to women. These kinds of revelations have challenged us to dig deep and consider what regulatory and legal measures are needed so that with AI we don't risk discriminatory and offensive results.

The robots are here and now it is our job to make the robots (AI) work for humans. This puts a spotlight on training and education. Companies and organizations need and will continue to need talent. The skills gap, whether severe or moderate will continue to increase because technologies will continue to evolve, increase in complexity and scale. Success moving forward depends on more than technology. Research done by the University Of South Florida's Business School in 2018 indicates that the top skills needed in the workplace through

2018 include: communications, problem solving, collaboration, ability to learn, creativity and resilience. It is not just about new algorithms and systems. It's ultimately about people. There is an ongoing need to train AI experts

We are obviously still trying to understand the huge changes facing the workforce and determine how and when training can be used to refocus and reposition humans. The magnitude of job loss in the coming decade will be extensive. The impact will reach far and deep. There are ethical implications to these cuts in the workforce. To use a well-worn analogy, implementation of AI will be like a snowball rolling down the hill. We have only begun to feel the impact. AI presents the possibility of blending the best of what machines can do with the best of what humans can do. Humans bring experience, judgment and empathy that coupled with AI augmentation will usher in new ways of working.

The threat to jobs is only partly about automation. Changes in the workplace will impact job rolls, skills, retraining and retaining workers. Companies and workers alike cannot be complacent. The AI revolution will affect all of us. Whether companies chose to hire from outside or retrain and reposition, continuing education and learning will play a huge role in our future. Ultimately, it is all about human talent.

AI can make workers better at their jobs, happier in their positions and more comfortable at home. It can empower people to make better decisions and increase job satisfaction. Both companies and individuals need sound strategies for talent development and continuing education. It's very important that we start now. The "arms race' for high quality technical talent has only begun. These people are not the only talent that is needed for success. Companies need leadership, executives that can speak and understand the technologies and workers that understand the limitations and uses of data and analytics. Although AI will help with automation and cut costs this is not the main or only purpose of cognitive technology. In many situations, AI is simple better and more efficient than humans at preforming a job function. In these cases where jobs are cognitively or task redundant, the positions will be replaced. In many more instances AI will stand alongside of people helping to make predictions, offering alternatives and interpreting information. Automation and augmentation will work hand in hand as we move forward to the agile workplace.

As you read this book there are a few things to remember. The nature of work is changing, and it is changing rapidly. Technological advancements in cognitive technologies, robotics, AI, machine learning or deep learning are with us and will impact all our lives. Our challenge is to embrace the changes and make them work in our favor. There is no going backwards. Technology never goes back. Much of the work that humans do today will be automated in the next decade. Many new jobs will open up and many new roles will need training and education. Get ready to learn and to continue to learn is the message of the future workplace. Machines and humans are already engaged in a collaborative workplace and more so every day. The future is robo-human. The robots are already here. Now is the time to embrace change and figure out how education, governments and companies prepare humans to be an active and productive part of it. Both technical skills and human skills will be needed in the workplace of the future. It's all about integration, augmentation and automation working hand in hand to provide humans with a better tomorrow.

Never underestimate the importance of human creativity and mental flexibility. Both will play a significant role in the workplace of tomorrow. We need to start to embrace change and teach these skills in the workplace and schools. Not just give them lip service, but incorporate affective intelligence, logic, ethics, values and judgement into all curriculums. Most educational institutions and organizations including the governments of the world are not adapting quickly enough to the changes that are being initiated now and those that lie ahead.

According to Robot Ready "The future of work is now and standing still is not an option. In order to shape the work of the future, organizations have a tremendous opportunity to redesign and cultivate this mindset of "both, and" earlier in the learning process (Robot Ready, 2019) . Learning needs to be ongoing and complete. This needs to encompass those skills needed in the workplace and those skills that support the continuing evolution of humans. Humans need to learn and continue to learn both technical skills and human skills. This learning will take place in the classroom, course room, on the job, in training and just about every other environment humans inhabit. Skills will need to be learned and relearned and more new skills will be added to the inventory of both traditional education and the workforce training. The skills gap needs to address those people looking for good work, those organizations looking for talent, educators and learning and development professionals looking to create pertinent programs. Continuing transformation and growth are the foundations of an agile workplace. The agile workplace will require radical change by institutions and organizations both in the way they do things and the mindset they bring to the tasks.

Get ready to learn. The future is not one of stagnation but of continued growth. This growth will require the ability to integrate technical and human skills and to continue to discover what is needed by the business, organization and humans in the workplace. Agile is the key to our future. How we get there is through continued improvement in cognitive technologies and continued human learning. Agile is about being awake, alert, vigilant and prepared. Those that can transform and navigate will look forward to a future where AI will bring vast improvements in productivity, freedom from boring repetitive work and improved quality of life.

ASK THE HARD QUESTIONS

- How will we use AI and how will we keep it from being abused?

- How will we measure success?

- How will we guard against disaster?

- How will AI affect the workplace? Your job? Future Jobs?

Bobbe Baggio was Associate Provost of the School of Adult and Graduate Education (SAGE) at Cedar Crest College in Allentown, PA. Her area of expertise is the integration of technologies to enhance human performance including adult and workplace learning. She was the Associate Dean of Graduate Programs and Online Learning at American University in Washington, D.C. and was previously Program Director of the MS program in Instructional Technology Management at La Salle University in Philadelphia, PA. Since 2002, she has been CEO of Advantage Learning Technologies, Inc. a company that provides programs, products and research for workplace learning. She believes that technologies are here to help everyone and to enhance human performance.

Bobbe is the author of five books, an engaging public speaker, strategic advisor and educator in the field of instructional technologies and learning. She was a consultant in learning and talent development for a global and virtually connected workforce. Her expertise draws upon her experience as a Fortune 100 IT manager, 20 years of consulting experience, and her doctoral studies in instructional design for online learning. Examples of clients include The Federal Reserve Bank, Pfizer, Novartis, Johnson & Johnson, University of Pennsylvania, DOD, PASSHE, Merck, BMS, KPMG, Siemens, Ticketmaster, IMG, Tyco Engineering, Fisher, Christiana Care Health System, Cisco and Adobe.

Index

CPSIA information can be obtained
at www.ICGtesting.com
Printed in the USA
LVHW020006140521
687425LV00017B/1648